H. C. Ketcham
Ph-363-3386-

Finding God Through the SANCTUARY

by Morris D. Lewis
and
LaVerne E. Tucker

Published by
THE QUIET HOUR, INC.
Redlands, California 92373

THE QUIET HOUR
A Radio, Television, Literature and Worldwide Mission Outreach

Presented by the Father, Son, and Grandson Broadcasting Team

Pastor J. L. Tucker, *Founder and Speaker*
Pastor LaVerne Tucker, *Director/Speaker*
Pastor Bill Tucker, *Director of Evangelism and Music Programming*

THE QUIET HOUR RADIOBROADCAST

is now released more than 400 times weekly throughout North and Central America, Europe, Southern Asia, and the Philippines.

SEARCH TELECAST

*with Pastor and Mrs. LaVerne Tucker
and Pastor and Mrs. Bill Tucker*

is now released weekly on more than 25 stations and repeater stations, plus more than 1000 cable systems.

This is the April/May 1982 Quiet Hour BOOK OF THE MONTH sent to those who contribute toward the support of The Quiet Hour radiobroadcasts, Search telecasts, and literature outreach.

THE QUIET HOUR
REDLANDS, CALIFORNIA 92373 USA

CONTENTS

PREFACE

Early in our ministry my wife, Alma, and I were privileged to be associated with Pastor Morris D. Lewis who has spent a lifetime studying the sanctuary.

Recently he was with us for a series of television programs and this book, *Finding God Through the Sanctuary*, is a compilation of the 13 presentations. Some of the conversation in question and answer form is retained in some chapters from the television series; in other chapters it is deleted. Those who may have made a recording of the television presentations will find the book version heavily edited, with helpful material added.

The entire series of television programs on the sanctuary is available in unedited form on half-inch VHS or Beta videocassettes. This book has also been narrated by Pastor LaVerne Tucker on audio cassettes and includes the songs sung by the Tucker Family Singers on this series of programs. Further information is found on pages 133-135.

The telecast series opened with the cameras on Pastor Morris Lewis standing in front of a large mural of the sanctuary in the wilderness of Sinai. My wife and I, our son, Pastor Bill Tucker, and on some programs, a guest or two, asked Pastor Lewis numerous questions. Guests included: Robert Dunn, Neva Coyle, and Jerry Friesen.
—*LaVerne E. Tucker*

Door of the   Altar of   The Laver   Door to the   Seven Golden   Table of   Altar of   The Veil   Ark and
Court   Burnt Offering   of washing   Holy Place   Candlesticks   Shewbread   Incense   Mercy Seat

THE SANCTUARY was built by Moses and the children of Israel while they camped at the base of Mt. Sinai. It was portable and moved from place to place. Later it was replaced by the Temple at Jerusalem built by Solomon, but planned by David.

THE TELEVISION SERIES, *Finding God Through The Sanctuary,* was recorded at The Quiet Hour studios. (Left to right) Pastor Morris D. Lewis, Pastor Bill Tucker, Alma Tucker, and Pastor LaVerne Tucker.

PASTOR MORRIS D. LEWIS, dressed as Aaron, the high priest, stands in front of a mural of the sanctuary holding a censer.

THE BREASTPLATE and precious stones, including the Urim and Thummim, worn by the high priest (See chapter 12).

Chapter 1
Christ's Relation to the Old Testament Sanctuary

PASTOR TUCKER: What is it? Where is it? Who is this man? Who does he represent? Why the colorful garment? Is this a special religious service? Does it have any meaning for you or for me? During the next 30 minutes we will find these answers and many, many more in our fascinating SEARCH FOR TRUTH. Today we have something very special for you.

Meet my friend, Pastor Morris D. Lewis. For more than 40 years he has made a careful study of the sanctuary. Dressed as Aaron, the high priest, Pastor Lewis will help us to know God better as he guides us through the sanctuary that God asked the children of Israel to build in the wilderness.

Pastor Lewis, does Christ in any way fit into this sanctuary?

PASTOR LEWIS: This is a picture of the mosaic sanctuary built by Moses and his associates about 1400 B.C. Christ is very distinctly featured in this particular building, as we find in John 2:13-20: "And the Jews' passover was at hand, and Jesus went up to Jerusalem, and found in the temple those that sold oxen and sheep and doves, and the changers of money sitting: . . . and said unto them that sold doves, Take these things hence; make not my Father's house an house of merchandise. . . . Then answered the Jews and said unto him, What sign shewest thou unto us, seeing that thou doest these things? Jesus answered and said unto them, Destroy this temple, and in three days I will raise it up. Then said the Jews, Forty and six years was this temple in building, and wilt thou rear it up in three days?''

The reference to the temple as His body is very distinctly related to the sanctuary of the Old Testament. Let us turn to Exodus 25:1 and 8: ''And the Lord spake unto Moses, saying, . . . And let them make me a sanctuary; that I may dwell among them.''

When the Lord said, ''Let *them* make me a sanctuary,'' He was referring to the children of Israel. And what they built is pictured in the mural on page 5. The children of Israel were migrating from Egypt to the Promised Land of Palestine. The sanctuary they built had to accommodate their moving from place to place.

Now God said, ''Let them make me a sanctuary.'' He instructed them to make the candlesticks, the table of showbread, the altar of incense, the veil, and the ark— all the pieces of furniture. From the words of Jesus, recorded in John, we can see a far deeper meaning in the command, ''Let them make me a sanctuary.'' It goes beyond this building to the Messiah, the Christ Himself. So when God said, ''Let them make me a sanctuary,'' He not only meant the sanctuary of the wilderness, and the more permanent temples at Jerusalem, but also the actual person of the Messiah Himself. So the children of Israel provided the material to structure the sanctuary, later the temples at Jerusalem, and these same people would make the contribution in the lineage of the coming Messiah.

Now we see the deeper meaning of the sanctuary

building. "You destroy this building and I will build it in three days." Christ was talking about the building of His person. Through the years the children of Israel were bringing the material of their lineage—father, son, father, son—the flesh that will constitute the Messiah, as is mentioned in the first chapter of Matthew. Here we see only one way in which the sanctuary points to the coming Messiah, but we shall see many more ways. That is what makes this whole subject of tremendous significance.

After each component of the sanctuary was built, the time came when the services of the sanctuary were to begin. "And the Lord spake unto Moses, saying, On the first day of the first month shalt thou set up the tabernacle of the tent of the congregation." Exodus 40:1, 2. When it was all set up God instructed Moses to take a golden bowl, put oil in it, and anoint every piece of furniture. "And thou shalt take the anointing oil, and anoint the tabernacle, and all that is therein, and shalt hallow it, and all the vessels thereof; and it shall be holy." Verse 9.

The very words used in this passage draw our attention to the close relationship of the Messiah and the sanctuary. The word *anoint* in Hebrew is *mashach*. And this word *mashach* transliterated into English would be the Messiah. When the high priest anointed each piece of furniture, we could say he Messiahed each piece of furniture. Every piece of furniture in the sanctuary has a deep meaning that pertains to an aspect of Christ's character.

PASTOR TUCKER: After being in Egypt as slaves for so many years, many of the children of Israel had such a little knowledge of God that they knew nothing about a coming Messiah. The whole plan of salvation had to be revealed to them. So God, through the sanctuary and its services, and even through the word *anoint* was revealing to His people His own person—the coming Anointed One, the Messiah!

PASTOR LEWIS: Yes, and this is why Christ could speak with such authority: "You destroy this temple and in three days I will raise it up." Though He was speaking of His own body, yet He realized that every piece of furniture and the entire structure had been built to reveal His character and person.

Now we come to the climax of the erecting of the sanctuary. "So Moses finished the work. Then a cloud covered the tent of the congregation, and the glory of the Lord filled the tabernacle. And Moses was not able to enter into the tent of the congregation, because the cloud abode thereon, and the glory of the Lord filled the tabernacle." Verses 33-35.

This is very important. This tabernacle represents Christ and this glory is the Shekinah—the divine presence of deity. This building was constructed with the materials that the people contributed, then God came into the building, which makes this building an incarnation—humanly built, divinely occupied.

This leads us right to the Messiah as a person, because when Christ came into the world it was an incarnation. The thoughts expressed in Acts 10:38 are very significant in relationship to the building and the act of anointing. "How God anointed Jesus of Nazareth with the Holy Ghost and with power: who went about doing good, and healing all that were oppressed of the devil; for God was with him."

When Christ was baptized the Holy Spirit came upon Him. "And John bare record, saying, I saw the Spirit descending from heaven like a dove, and it abode upon him. And I knew him not: but he that sent me to baptize with water, the same said unto me, Upon whom thou shalt see the Spirit descending, and remaining on him, the same is he which baptizeth with the Holy Ghost." John 1:32, 33. In reality when Moses anointed with oil (symbolic of the Holy Spirit) each piece of furniture in the sanctuary, the glory of the Lord came into that building. This pointed forward to that time when the Messiah would be anointed by the Spirit at His baptism, and the glory of God would come into the building—His person!

"And the Word was made flesh, and dwelt among us, (and we beheld his glory, the glory as of the only begotten of the Father,) full of grace and truth." John 1:14. So when Christ took on flesh (by the contribution of the people of Israel) and came into the world, then the glory of the Lord came into His life or into His temple.

PASTOR BILL TUCKER: Did the Jewish people really accept Christ as the Messiah?

PASTOR LEWIS: I would have to say that most of them did not. But there were some who did. Notice the experience described in John 1:40: "One of the two which heard John speak, and followed him was Andrew, Simon Peter's brother. He first findeth his own brother Simon, and saith unto him, We have found the Messias, which is, being interpreted, the Christ."

If you have a marginal reading, for the word *Christ* it says *anointed.* In this passage we have Hebrew, Greek, and English. The *Messiah* is Hebrew. *Christ* is the Greek word, and *anointed* the English.

In the conversation with Christ the woman at the well said to Him, "I know that Messias cometh, which is called Christ: when he is come, he will tell us all things." John 4:25. She recognized the Messiah was coming and made reference to it. Now notice the 29th verse: "Come, see a man, which told me all things that ever I did: is not this the Christ?" She used Hebrew and Greek in one verse and only Greek in the other.

13

ALMA: Are there other scripture passages that show a definite relationship between the Old Testament temple and the New Testament Christ?

PASTOR LEWIS: Yes, there are and they reveal a most striking relationship. Christ distinctly understood who He was, what He was to do, and how His life would be related to this building. "These words spake Jesus, and lifted up his eyes to heaven, and said, Father, the hour is come; glorify thy Son, that thy Son also may glorify thee." John 17:1. Now you recall the word "glorify" is in relationship to the sanctuary. When they anointed it the divine power of deity came into the building. Here He is making the same observation. "The hour is come; glorify thy Son." Now verse 4: "I have glorified thee on the earth: I have finished the work which thou gavest me to do." Now you recall in the Old Testament it said after a time they finished the structure. Now Christ is saying, I have finished the meaning of the structure, I have taken humanity, which these people contributed to the building, I have now brought this to absolute glorification, to the perfection of the quality of the Son of God.

PASTOR TUCKER: What does that have to do then with me, with every one of our viewers—our readers? What relationship do we find in all of this? Here are the materials; here is Christ in the temple. What does it have to do with me?

PASTOR LEWIS: If we relate ourselves to Christ as our personal Saviour, then our person becomes a sanctuary; and this further extends the meaning of the building and brings it very pertinent to us that it is all accomplished through the fact that Christ became flesh, built the sanctuary, and glorified it by manifesting the character of heaven. It would be well to underline in your own Bible these inspired words in 1 Corinthians 3:16, 17: "Know ye not that ye are the temple of God, and that the Spirit of God dwelleth in you?"

PASTOR TUCKER: What a beautiful thought! You and I are temples for the indwelling of the Holy Spirit. God said, "Let them make me a sanctuary"—a temple—"that I may dwell among them." Friend, God wants to live in you. Is there a hungar in your heart? There is in mine. Right now as you read the words of the song, More of You, commit your life to our wonderful Saviour. More and more of Him is what we need.

MORE OF YOU

I'm not trying to find just some new frame of mind
   That will change my old point of view,
For I've been through it all,
   Deep inside nothing's changed, I'm not new.
I'm not seeking a gift or emotional lift,
   But one thing I'm longing to do—Is to lift up my cup
   And let You fill it up with just You.

More of You . . . more of You,
   I've had all, but what I need—just more of You.
Of things I've had my fill—and yet I hunger still,
   Empty and bare, Lord hear my prayer for more of You.

I have searched all around in the husks that abound,
   But I find no nourishment there,
Now my strength's almost gone and I feel the pull of
     despair.
Yet my thirst drives me on—and I stumble along,
   Over ground so barren and dry,
For the spring's just ahead—living water, "Lord,
     fill me," I cry.

—Selected

Chapter 2
Christ Is the Door

PASTOR TUCKER: There must be a deep significance to the beautiful garments worn by the high priest of the sanctuary.

PASTOR LEWIS: Yes. There is deep meaning in these multicolors of his garments. The upper jacket is most colorful with a mixture of red, purple, and blue colors. Under the jacket is a garment entirely of blue with bells and pomegranates on it. Beneath this is a long white garment that almost reaches the ground with blue ribbon around the bottom. These three aspects of the garment correspond with the three sections of the sanctuary.

The white wall around the sanctuary has a blue border on the bottom just as the blue on the garment. The holy place of the sanctuary has a distinct relationship to the entire blue garment. The most holy place where God's presence dwells corresponds to the very colorful blue, purple, and scarlet ephod. These same colors of the ephod are in the door of the sanctuary. And today we want to study that.

Let's take our Bibles right now and open to Exodus 38:18: "And the hanging for the gate of the court was needlework, of blue, and purple, and scarlet, and fine twined linen." Well it is obvious from this text that the door was made from fine linen and dyed blue, purple, and scarlet. This has a very significant meaning in the life of Christ.

God directed Moses to teach the children of Israel that each one was to wear a border of blue on their garments. And for what reason? Notice what we read here in Numbers 15:38, 39: "Speak unto the children of Israel, and bid them that they make them fringes in the borders of their garments throughout their generations, and that they put upon the fringe of the borders a ribband of blue: And it shall be unto you for a fringe, that ye may look upon it, and remember all the commandments of the Lord, and do them."

It is significant that in the Hebrew language, the word for "blue," as it is stated here and in the door, is *kalah* or *kaloth* which means righteousness, virtue, or perfection. So when God said they were to put the blue in the door it indicatively meant righteousness and virtue of the law of God. So you look upon it and remember the righteous character of God.

Jesus said, as recorded here in John 10:9: "I am the door: by me if any man enter in, he shall be saved." It is very interesting that the individual should recognize that the door at the entrance of the sanctuary, the outer gate, represents Christ. This being so, the colors must have a direct distinctive interpretation in His person. That is what we will find in the revelation of Scripture.

In Matthew 14:35, 36 we see how this is revealed in the life of Christ. "And when the men of that place had knowledge of him, they sent out into all that country round about, and brought unto him all that were diseased." I'd like to emphasize this particular fact: "When the men in that place *had knowledge of Christ,* they sent out into all the country round about, and brought unto him all that were diseased.

17

"And besought him that they might only touch the hem of his garment: and as many as touched were made perfectly whole." In Hebrew, the word for "perfectly whole," is the same word for "blue." So when the people touched the hem, which obviously in His case had a blue hem or ribbon around the bottom of it, they became perfectly well of whatever disease they had. The text says that they had knowledge of Him. There was a connection between the blue hem of His garment and the blue in the sanctuary door. Really that door of the entrance of the sanctuary represents Christ. The decision to go through the door of the sanctuary was of utmost importance.

In Proverbs 23:7 you remember this passage: "For as he thinketh in his heart, so is he." In other words, as a man thinketh, so is he. This is correct psychologically. Whatever a person thinks in his mind constantly will finally show up in his conduct, his character. It is significant that the word "think" in that particular text is the same word for the sanctuary door. When Christ says, "I am the door," He is asking the individual to think upon Him and in Him experience Christ's righteousness. This is what the blue in the door teaches the worshiper.

But what about the other colors? The color of red in the door of the sanctuary? Let's turn to that beautiful passage in Revelation 1:5, 6. We read, "And from Jesus Christ, who is the faithful witness, and the first begotten of the dead, and the prince of the kings of the earth. Unto him that loved us, and washed us from our sins in his own blood." This red stripe in the sanctuary door, the outer gate, represents Christ's blood shed on Calvary for our sins. The Hebrews have a way of symbolizing the magnificent aspects of the sanctuary and their meaning as they pertain to Christ.

In Isaiah 63:1-3 is a beautiful prediction of Christ. "Who is this that cometh from Edom" the scripture says. The word "Edom" is related to the word "adam." It is just a matter of vocalization of the vowels. In Hebrew the word "adam" means dirt, obviously a red-hue dirt. So God took some of the dirt, "adam," and made a man and called him "Adam." The latter part of that word "dam" has reference to red or blood. So "who is this that comes from Edom, . . . from Bozrah?"

Bozrah was the area in Palestine where the very best grapes grew. So anybody knew that when you referred to Bozrah, you were referring to the best grape vineyards in all of Palestine. So our text reads, "Who is this that comes from Bozrah? . . . travelling in the greatness of his strength? I that speak in righteousness, mighty to save." This refers to the blue in the coloring.

"I have trodden the winepress alone; and of the people there was none with me: . . . their blood shall be sprinkled upon my garments." If a person were in a wine vat stomping the grapes, in time the red juice would splash on his garments. So the people said, "Who is this that comes from Bozrah with grape juice splashed on his garments? He who is mighty to save" refers to Christ. So the red in this door of the sanctuary refers to the grape juice or the blood that Christ shed for the sins of the people. This is very important.

In the garden of Gethsemane, when Christ took the sins of the world upon Himself, He must suffer the consequence of those transgressions. He took the sins in His mind and He wrestled with them in His mind because they were going to separate Him from God and actually kill Him. In His mind, Christ suffered the consequences of sin.

This red stripe in the door of the sanctuary pointed forward to all this agony and suffering of our precious Saviour. In His great love, Christ held on to the human race until their sins took Him down to an eternal death. The blood oozing from the wounds, the crown of thorns

19

on His head, the nails in His hands and feet, and the spear in his side were all foretold by the red stripe in the sanctuary door.

When a person came to the door of the sanctuary he was to contemplate what that door meant to him and as he looked upon the red stripe, he began to think of the coming Saviour who would shed His blood for him, who would pay the penalty of eternal death for Him.

As he saw the blue in that door he would begin to think of the righteousness of God that would cover his sinful nature. And as the sinner stepped through the door of the sanctuary, it meant that he was accepting by faith the righteousness as well as the shed blood of the Saviour to come.

Oh my friend, what a lesson God gave to His people way back there in the Jewish sanctuary. Aren't you glad that He loves you today with an everlasting love? And I pray that as you continue the study of these thrilling themes of the sanctuary, your love, your appreciation for our Saviour, and your desire for His righteousness to cover you will be more intense, more complete than ever before. May God bless you as you reach out to Him just now and find salvation full and complete and free.

The purple color in the door also has deep meaning. In Judges 8:26 we are told that the kings wore purple robes. This purple robe was dyed from a solution taken from the bodies of little shellfish in the Mediterranean and it was hard to come by. They had to get bushels of these shellfish to get a quantity enough to dye any sizable garment. But when they did it was the most gorgeous purple you ever laid your eyes on and it was a fast color. But only the kings could afford it. Here is an important lesson in the interpretation of Hebrew symbols.

During Christ's trial a purple robe was placed on Him.

The Bible says: "Then Pilate therefore took Jesus, and scourged him. And the soldiers platted a crown of thorns, and put it on his head, and they put on him a purple robe. And said, Hail, King of the Jews! and they smote him with their hands." John 19:1, 2.

These soldiers were mocking Him. On trial Christ had said He was the King of the Jews and Pilate interrogated Him on that matter. So the soldiers, to mock Him, said if He claims to be a King, He has to have a robe. So the purple robe was put on Him to mock Him. But it really fitted His life at that particular juncture.

What we must see now is the fact that Christ said, "I am the door." He could also say, "I am the blue in the door," which is His righteousness. "I am the red in the door," which is His death. And these two colors put together makes the color of kings—purple. This is the great reward of all saints. The apostle Paul said, "I have finished my course, I have kept the faith: Henceforth there is laid up for me a crown of righteousness." 2 Timothy 4:7, 8.

The purple stripe in the sanctuary door refers to the reward of all the redeemed of this earth who accept Christ and go through the first door of the sanctuary. This door depicts the great basic concepts of Christ; His righteousness that you receive by going through that door, His death upon the cross for your sins by going through that door, and that He will bring you all the way through the sanctuary and finally make you a king.

As recorded in Revelation 3:21, Christ stated: "To him that overcometh will I grant to sit with me on my throne, even as I also overcame, and am set down with my Father in his throne." The purple color in the first door pointed the worshiper forward to the day of rewards when God is going to welcome the redeemed of this earth to sit with Him on His throne. The purple color in the second door and the third door again points to the fact that Christ will welcome the saints to sit with Him and rule as kings throughout the ceaseless ages of eternity.

All this may seem to the casual reader as an exercise in works. However, this is not so. This is an act of faith. "And when they were come, and had gathered the church together, they rehearsed all that God had done with them, and how he had opened the door of faith unto the Gentiles." Acts 14:27. It distinctly says Gentiles—people without hope and without God in the world. God has opened a door—the door of faith—for these people. Now you recognize that faith is an aspect of thinking. The word *faith* comes from the Greek word which has to do with thinking and believing.

A person thinks of Christ and believes that He fulfills all that these colors represent. Blue—he has faith in Christ's righteousness. Red—he has faith that Christ has died for his sins. Purple—he has faith that Christ will open to him the throne of God eternally. When a person begins this relationship with Christ by faith, he steps from the area of Gentile into the realm of God's perfect character.

To put this all together in a realistic experience, there is a particular story related in Matthew 9:20-22. A woman was ill with a continual hemorrhage and she sought help from the physicians, but her illness continued. She learned of Christ and His power to heal. She determined to find Him and see if her sickness could be healed. When she saw Him and saw His white garment with the blue ribbon around the bottom, she remembered what that blue represented—reverence and respect of God's law. The more she followed Him and heard Him preach and teach, the more she was convinced that the blue ribbon around His garment was exactly what she needed—a power to restore her from sin. In her mind she said, "If I touch the hem of His garment . . . (If I can only touch that blue ribbon around the bottom of His garment) I will be made whole." One day she found Him in a crowded street and moved up behind and touched Him.

Immediately Christ said, "Who touched me?" The disciples said, "Well, who hasn't touched you in this crowded street?" Jesus said, "I perceive that righteousness or virtue has gone out of my life." In Hebrew this word *virtue* is the same word as used for *blue.*

My appeal to you today is this: Accept Jesus as your righteousness. Accept Him as your Saviour. Accept Him as your eternal reward. Know the eternal joys that He has planned for you. Today He longs to touch your life and make you whole. Let Him do it now!

HE TOUCHED ME

Shackled by a heavy burden, 'neath a load of guilt and shame
Then the hand of Jesus touched me and now I am no longer
the same!

He touched me, oh He touched me
And oh the joy that floods my soul!
Something happened and now I know,
He touched me and made me whole!

Since I met this blessed Saviour, since He cleansed and made
me whole
I will never cease to praise Him, I'll shout it while eternity rolls!
—*William J. Gaither*

Chapter 3
Behold the Lamb

The next day John seeth Jesus coming unto him, and saith, Behold the Lamb of God, which taketh away the sin of the world." John 1:29. The great prophet, John the Baptist, recognized that Christ represented the lamb of the Old Testament sanctuary service. In the symbols of the sanctuary, the sins of the world were portrayed as removed and the sinner forgiven by the sacrifice of the lamb.

God carefully pointed out each detail in the sanctuary services and the importance of the sacrifice of the lamb. "If his offering be a burnt sacrifice of the herd, let him offer a male without blemish: he shall offer it of his own voluntary will at the door of the tabernacle of the congregation before the Lord." Leviticus 1:3.

The lamb was offered on the altar in the courtyard before the tabernacle door. There is one particular statement made in this text that makes the lamb applicable to Christ in a very distinct way. "Let him offer a male without blemish." John obviously recognized Christ to be that Lamb without blemish and said: "Behold the Lamb of God, which taketh away the sin of the world."

In Leviticus 3:8 we read: "And he shall lay his hand

upon the head of his offering, and kill it before the tabernacle of the congregation: and Aaron's sons shall sprinkle the blood thereof round about upon the altar."

When a lamb was offered as a sacrifice for sin, the blood was sprinkled upon the altar, particularly on the horns of the altar and was poured out at the base. But notice one particular feature: the man "shall lay his hand upon the head" of the lamb and confess his sins. So he would convey his sins from his person to the animal by placing his hands upon the animal. Then he himself would kill it, indicating that his sin is what caused the death of the lamb. The priest in behalf of the man would take the blood and begin to officiate. The man was on the north side of the altar, which was next to God "in the north of the sanctuary" as the symbolism is made.

You may ask, Why did they have to kill the poor lamb and then sprinkle the blood on the altar? God said it should be a lamb. The lamblike characteristics of meekness and gentleness would best represent Christ in submitting Himself as a sacrifice. Here is a Bible verse that will answer your question, Jeremiah 17:1: "The sin of Judah is written with a pen of iron, and with the point of a diamond: it is graven upon the table of their heart, and upon the horns of your altars."

In Scripture symbols, iron is a symbol of corruption. When building the temple in Jerusalem the builders were instructed that iron tools were not to be used at the site of the sanctuary. Iron was a symbol of sin and it was never to be used in the structure of this building. The scripture says that the "sin of Judah is written with a pen of iron, and with the point of a diamond."

Where is the writing? "It is graven upon the table of their heart, and upon the horns of your altars." He is speaking here of writing the sins on the horns of the

25

altar. The priest took the blood from the lamb and put it on the horns of the altar. It was inscribing the sins of the man by his hands placed on the lamb and finally to the blood on the horns. It was written as with a diamond point, with an iron pen. Now in writing it on the horns of the altar, in reality it was on the table of their heart—their mind. So you see the tremendous implication here is that your sins are written in your mind and to show that they are written indelibly, it is an iron pen with a diamond point.

Long before the sanctuary was built in the wilderness, the altar was in use. One of the places where this altar is distinctly mentioned in a very beautiful but graphic way is during the life of Abraham. God said to him: "Take now thy son, thine only son Isaac, whom thou lovest, and get thee into the land of Moriah: and offer him there for a burnt offering upon one of the mountains which I will tell thee of." Genesis 22:2.

Abraham had been tested before and failed. Now God tested him again to see if he really trusted God. We must remember that the miraculous birth of Isaac is a type of the coming of Christ. So He said, "Take this son, whom thou lovest, northward." At that time they were living in Beersheba which was three days journey to Moriah. In that marvelous book *Patriarchs and Prophets,* written by Ellen G. White, I find this heart-touching commentary:

"Day was approaching, and he must be on his journey. . . . He went to the place where Isaac lay sleeping the deep, untroubled sleep of youth and innocence. For a moment the father looked upon the dear face of his son, then turned tremblingly away. He went to the side of Sara, who was also sleeping. Should he awaken her, that she might once more embrace her child? Should he tell her of God's requirement? He longed to unburden his heart to her, and share with her this terrible responsibility; but he was restrained by the fear that she might hinder him. Isaac was her joy and pride; her life was bound up in him, and the mother's love might refuse the sacrifice.

"Abraham at last summoned his son, telling him of the command to offer sacrifice upon a distant mountain. Isaac had often gone with his father to worship. . . . The preparations for the journey were quickly completed. The wood was made ready, and put upon the ass, and with two men-servants they set forth.

"Side by side the father and the son journeyed in silence. . . . That day—the longest that Abraham had ever experienced—dragged slowly to its close. While his son and the young men were sleeping, he spent the night in prayer, still hoping that some heavenly messenger might come to say that the trial was enough, that the youth might return unharmed to his mother. But no relief came to his tortured soul. Another long day, another night of humiliation and prayer, while ever the command that was to leave him childless was ringing in his ears. Satan was near to whisper doubts and unbelief; but Abraham resisted his suggestions. As they were about to begin the journey of the third day, the patriarch, looking northward, saw the promised sign, a cloud of glory hovering over Mount Moriah, and he knew that the voice which had spoken to him was from heaven."

Listen to this. Here is genuine faith. Abraham "did not murmur against God, but strengthened his soul by dwelling upon the evidences of the Lord's goodness and faithfulness. This son had been unexpectedly given; and had not He who bestowed the precious gift a right to recall His own? Then faith repeated the promise, 'In Isaac shall thy seed be called,'—a seed numberless as the grains of sand upon the shore. Isaac was the child of a miracle, and could not the power that gave him life restore it? Looking beyond that which was seen, Abraham grasped the divine word, 'accounting that God was able to raise him up, even from the dead.' Hebrews 11:19. Yet none but God could understand how great was the father's sacrifice in yielding up his son to death." Pages 148-150.

Abraham desired that no one but God should witness the parting scene. He asked his servants to remain behind, saying, "I and the lad will go yonder and worship, and come again to you." Genesis 22:5.

Now notice verse 6: "And Abraham took the wood of the burnt offering, and laid it upon Isaac his son; and he took the fire in his hand, and a knife; and they went both of them together." Isaac is a type of Christ and this wood represents the cross of Calvary. And this is the same mountain that Christ climbed nineteen hundred years later. This mountain has a most unusual name—Moriah—which means Jehovah is watching, beholding, and He sees.

As the father and son climbed toward the mountain summit in silence, the boy wondered where they would find a lamb. Finally Isaac asked: "My father: . . . Behold the fire and the wood: but where is the lamb for a burnt offering?"

What faith! "God will provide," because God is watching. God is beholding and He will see to it. The Lord will take care of it. Together they walk on to the place of sacrifice and build the altar and place the wood upon it. Now the moment of truth arrives. With tears in his voice, Abraham revealed God's message to his son. Isaac is struck with terror and amazement, but he does not run away. Willingly he submits to God's command and encourages his father to bind him to the altar.

In the book of Psalms it says, "He was bound to the horns of the altar." Now we are back to the symbol here in the sanctuary. The word "horn" (in Hebrew) is on the four corners of the altar in the sanctuary. That is where the blood is placed. "Horn" in Hebrew means power, strength. So the sacrifice, Isaac, was bound to the horn because the sin, the life, has a hold upon him that he will not be able to get away. "His own iniquities shall take [hold of] the wicked himself, and he shall be holden with the cords of his sins." Proverbs 5:22.

When Isaac was placed on the altar the cords bound him to the horns of it because he was representing Christ who had the sins of the world laid on Him. These sins would bind Him to the altar for a sacrifice because the penalty of sin is death and He will be bound on this altar until He fulfills the requisite for sin.

Now you see why the lamb is killed and why the blood is put on the horns of the altar. Sin has power in our life to take us to destruction. So Isaac permitted himself to be bound. Shaking the emotion, Abraham offers the sacrificial prayer. The last words of love are spoken and the last embrace given. Just as he raises the knife to plunge it into the heart of his son, his arm is stopped. An angel of God called to him out of heaven, and said, "Abraham, Abraham: . . . Lay not thine hand upon the lad, neither do thou any thing unto him: for now I know that thou fearest God, seeing thou hast not withheld thy son, thine only son from me. And Abraham lifted up his eyes, and looked, and behold behind him a ram caught in the thicket." Genesis 22:11-13.

Just as Abraham was going to slay his own son, the angel said, Stop! Stop! And he turned and saw a ram caught in a thicket—thorns which represent sin. And the Lord said, "Now take the ram and put him in the place of your son." Abraham might have said, "God, why are You making this change?" And God is saying by this action: "Your son will not have to die but My sacrifice will die in the place of your son." Abraham might have said, "Oh, I see. I should take my son off and put on the altar a sacrifice which represents Christ. Now I see why the great requisite for sin. The eradicating of sin will come from Christ and not from any sacrifice I present, even my son."

Now we can understand why the altar—that place—was called Moriah. It means "I see God." He wanted Abraham to see, to understand what it means to offer your own son to die for the sins of the world. Now Abraham understood. "Now I see what God is doing. He is putting His Son in the place of mine to die on Calvary."

To add to the significance and relationship between the altar on Mount Moriah and the altar in the sanctuary court, let us read the story found in 2 Chronicles 3:1. "Then Solomon began to build the house of the Lord at Jerusalem in mount Moriah, where the Lord appeared unto David his father, in the place that David had prepared in the threshingfloor of Ornan the Jebusite." David had sinned in numbering Israel. As a result the land of Israel was smitten with pestilence, which destroyed seventy thousand in Israel. David prayed that the slaughter be stopped and it was.

The destroying angel stood upon Mount Moriah in the threshingfloor of Ornan. David went there and built an altar to the Lord, "and offered burnt offerings and peace offerings, and called upon the Lord; and he answered him from heaven by fire upon the altar of burnt offering. 1 Chronicles 21:26. The spot upon which the altar was erected became known as holy ground. It was here that Abraham had built an altar to offer up his son and later became the site of the temple erected by Solomon.

The sanctuary built in the wilderness of Sinai was moved from place to place. But when it was replaced with the temple built by Solomon, the altar was on the same spot where Abraham had offered Isaac and the same place where David had offered that special sacrifice on the altar he erected at the threshingfloor of Ornan. And all these altars erected for the worship of God from Adam's day to the crucifixion of Christ pointed forward to that supreme sacrifice by the Son of God on Calvary. "Behold the Lamb of God, which taketh away the sin of the world."

Chapter 4
Christ in the Court

PASTOR TUCKER: Friend, "whatever your worries, anxieties and trials, spread out your life before the Lord." You can find God and His way through the sanctuary. "Your spirit will be braced for endurance. The way will be open for you to disentangle yourself from embarrassment and difficulty. The weaker and more helpless that you know yourself to be, the stronger will you become in God's strength. Let Him be your helper today." —Ellen G. White, *The Desire of Ages,* page 329.

Pastor Lewis, how is it that Christ, being of the tribe of Judah, is able to minister in the court in the sanctuary?

PASTOR LEWIS: Notice the beautiful sentiment expressed by the psalmist in regards to the court of the sanctuary in Psalms 65:4. "Blessed is the man whom thou choosest, and causest to approach unto thee, that he may dwell in thy courts: we shall be satisfied with the goodness of thy house, even of thy holy temple." Now notice that it says in particularly that God would cause the person to approach unto Him. The sanctuary is the visual aid that God gave the people of Israel to illustrate how they may approach unto God. And of course, the first step is into the court as we have indicated here by the white fence made out of linen that went clear around the sanctuary. A person must enter into the court, and when he does he begins his approach unto God. Christ Himself had a great deal to say of this experience. Notice His statement—"When I was daily with you in the temple, ye stretched forth no hands against me: but this is your hour, and the power of darkness. Then took they him and led him, and brought him into the high priest's house. And Peter followed afar off." Luke 22:53. When Christ was at Jerusalem He spent a great deal of time in the court of the sanctuary ministering to the people who came into this area. Now you recall that Christ was of the tribe of Judah and was not necessarily the priest. But He was allowed as a rabbi to come into the court.

ALMA: Well, Pastor Lewis, how would a person be especially blessed who came into the court?

PASTOR LEWIS: The word "bless" is a very significant word and is used many times by the Hebrews. Often it is used in relationship with coming into the court. In Acts 3:26 we read, "Unto you first God, having raised up his Son Jesus, sent him to bless you, in turning away every one of you from his iniquities." Now this may seem to be a very casual text that God would send Christ to "bless you in turning away every one from his iniquities." A basic principle of human conduct is: What a person sows, he will reap; what measure he administers to others will be that which returns to him. That is to say that all human conduct comes out of your past life. What you did yesterday is quite likely what you will do today. This is the law of God's Ten Commandments that your conduct will repeat. This truth is clearly portrayed in Proverbs 5:22. "His own iniquities shall take the wicked himself and he shall be holden with the cords of his sins." Now what would you think that that means?

PASTOR BILL TUCKER: Didn't we take this up in a previous study when the sacrifice was bound to the horns of the altar by cords? He is bound by sin.

PASTOR LEWIS: That's it. You see he is bound. There is a very interesting text in First Corinthians, chapter fifteen that is very helpful on this very point we are discussing. "O death, where is thy sting? O grave, where is thy victory? The sting of death is sin and the strength of sin is the law." 1 Corinthians 15:55, 56. This signifies that the law of sin is going to bind the person to the altar, which typifies the cross of Calvary. So sin binds you to death by a process of law. "The wages of sin is death." Romans 6:23.

"The wages of sin is death." Romans 6:23.

If a person lives a life of selfishness, a life of sin yesterday, he's going to be bound to live the same thing today. And every time he does, this cord becomes stronger and stronger by repetition until he is really bound and will never get away. Now for a person to break that binding and be loosed from sin is a tremendous event. Only by the divine power of God could it be accomplished. So when it says God will send His Son to bless you in turning you away from your sins this is one of the great problems of the plan of salvation. It is not easily done! But if the person approaches God through the court, he will be blessed. In the court he will be turned from his sins. The altar in the court represents the cross of Calvary. And in as much as Christ took the sins of the whole world upon Him and He was bound to fulfill the requirements of the law and the consequence of sin, it took Him down to eternal destruction. "For the love of Christ constraineth us; because we thus judge, that if one died for all, then were all dead." 2 Corinthians 5:14.

The observation Paul makes is plain—if Christ died for every person, then in a sense every person was dead in sin. "And he is the propitiation for our sins: and not for ours only, but also for the sins of the whole world." 1 John 2:2.

34

Now you see this text amplifies the fact that if Christ died for all, all were dead. Now the point in the sanctuary that is applicable to this text is that Christ became the propitiation for our sins. That word "propitiation" in the Hebrew language refers to the lid on this ark where the final atonement will be made. But we are thinking today about the court. As the individual comes into the court he will be blessed. That is, he will be turned away from his sins. So the turning away from sins takes place in the court but the final atonement for sin takes place in the most holy place and we will get to that in a future study.

The Bible says, "Because the law worketh wrath: for where no law is, there is no transgression." Romans 4:15. The prophet here has changed. He could have said where sin is but he used the word "wrath." But the word "wrath," and the word "sin" are the same in the Hebrew language. But the word "wrath" is good because we want to use it in regards to this altar of burnt offerings. The law works wrath and brings the person into condemnation. Although the law does work wrath, God has made a provision to switch it from the individual who commmits the sin and brings wrath to Christ who made the atonement.

Now there is a particular text that introduces the court in a very beautiful way found in 2 Chronicles 6:13. Here is the delineation of the Davidic temple. When Solomon had finished the structure, the greatest of all physical temples, he built a platform in the court. It was much, much larger than this picture shows with the Mosaic sanctuary. He built a platform and from there offered the dedicatory prayer for this building. And you can imagine it would be a very significant part in the great program of dedication. "For Solomon had made a brasen scaffold, of five cubits long, and five cubits broad, and three cubits high, and had set it in the midst of the court: and upon it he stood, and kneeled down upon his knees'' and he began to pray. 2 Chronicles 6:13.

The word "court" in this area where the platform was in the Hebrew language is *azarah*. This means a help-meet. See how that word is used in relation to Adam and Eve. "And the Lord said, It is not good that the man should be alone; I will make him an help meet for him." Genesis 2:18. Now what would you, under the circumstance of Adam and the creation of his wife, and she was a beautiful woman, what is conveyed by the idea that Eve would be a helpmeet for Adam?

PASTOR TUCKER: A good helper.

ALMA: She would be affectionate; one who would make life much, much more enjoyable and easier.

PASTOR LEWIS: Christ assumes the same position as a helpmeet for the individual. "What profit is there in my blood, when I go down to the pit? Shall the dust praise thee? shall it declare thy truth? Hear, O Lord, and have mercy upon me: Lord, be thou my helper." Psalm 30:9, 10.

In place of the word "helper" put the word "court," for they have the same meaning. "Lord, be thou my court" or "be thou my helpmeet." So the moment the person steps into the court of the sanctuary God is his helpmeet, his aid and will lead him step by step finally to the throne of God. So the moment he steps into this court area, God puts His arms around him so to speak and says, "Look, I will be your helpmeet. I will see you through."

Did you notice the reading of the text? "What would it profit if my blood were used?" Well, if the sinner used his own blood to pay his atonement, he would be forever destroyed. But God is going to supply His blood in place of the sinner's blood and thus put His arms around him and aid him. Now the beautiful text I want you to see is Numbers 18:5. To me this is where the court comes into its apex of revelation in the Christian's personal life. "And ye shall keep the charge of the sanctuary, and the charge of the altar: that there be no wrath any more upon the children of Israel."

Now that is a magnificent text. In as much, now, as Christ has died for all, has suffered the wrath of every sinner, now the sinner has come into a relationship with Christ, the Helpmeet. Christ says to him in effect, "I will take your sin and prevent the ill effect on your conduct to come on Me so that you will be relieved from it." The prophet charges the priest serving in the court to have charge of the altar of burnt offerings and officiate in taking the sins from the person, putting them upon the altar so that the ill effects of those sins do not cause them wrath, destruction and discomfort. Now this is what God is doing in the life of the Christian every single day in the court. So this court gives immediate help and Christ puts His arms as a helpmeet around the individual and says, "I'll take care of you. I will lead you on to the throne."

Near the Cross

Jesus, keep me near the cross,
There a precious fountain—
Free to all, a healing stream
Flows from Calv'ry's mountain.

In the cross, in the cross
Be my glory ever.
'Til my raptured soul shall find
Rest beyond the river.

Alas, and did my Saviour bleed
And did my Sovereign die.
Would He devote that sacred head
For such a worm as I?

At the cross, at the cross
Where I first saw the light,
And the burden of my heart rolled away.
It was there by faith I received my sight,
And now I am happy all the day.

Near the cross I'll watch and wait,
Hoping, trusting ever;
'Til I reach the golden strand
Just beyond the river.

In the cross, in the cross
Be my glory ever.
'Til my raptured soul shall find
Rest beyond the river.

Chapter 5
Entering the Holy Place

In our last study we found the spiritual meaning of entering by faith into the courtyard of the sanctuary. Today we will begin to understand how a person by faith moves on into the sanctuary—into the holy place and later into the most holy place.

By inspiration the apostle Paul has given us an observation about the sanctuary in Hebrews 6:1. "Therefore leaving the principles of the doctrine of Christ, let us go on to perfection; not laying again the foundation of repentance from dead works and of faith toward God, and of the doctrine of baptism." Now, what he is saying is, let's not lay again the foundation doctrines of baptism, repentance, and acceptance of Christ which is represented by the first door, but let us move on into the sanctuary for "the way of God is in the sanctuary." Psalm 77:13. And that is what these studies are trying to bring out—God's way revealed in the sanctuary!

PASTOR LEWIS: The 118th Psalm will help us understand God's way in the sanctuary. "Open to me the gates of righteousness: I will go into them, and I will praise the Lord; This gate of the Lord, into which the righteous shall enter." Psalm 118:19, 20.

Notice that "righteousness" is mentioned twice. It speaks of righteousness in reference to the gate, and righteousness for those who go through. Those who have gone through the first door have accepted Christ as Saviour, received His righteousness, and moved on through the sanctuary into the holy place.

PASTOR TUCKER: But in actuality no one other than the priest can go in to the holy place.

PASTOR LEWIS: Yes, that is true. But the priest now assumes the position of the individual. Although we are talking about geographically moving through the holy place, at the same time we are talking about the Christian's growing relationship with God. So the question is: Having gone through this door what next step should I take into righteousness? Paul said, "Let's go on to perfection" for God's way is in the sanctuary!

This move we must clearly understand. Notice David's thinking at the end of his life. "But who am I, and what is my people, that we should be able to offer so willingly after this sort? for all things come of thee, and of thine own have we given thee." 1 Chronicles 29:14. Anything we give to God, He has first given to us. This is an important point that David is making. We don't give something to God that we ourselves have developed. What we give Him, He has first given us.

"O Lord our God, all this store that we have prepared to build thee an house for thine holy name cometh of thine hand, and is all thine own. I know also, my God, that thou triest the heart, and hast pleasure in uprightness. As for me, in the uprightness of mine heart I have willingly offered all these things: and now have I seen with joy thy people which are present here, to offer willingly unto thee." You see, he is talking about their contribution of gold, jewels, etc. to build the sanctuary. "O Lord God of Abraham, Isaac, and of Israel, our fathers, keep this forever in the imagination of the thoughts of the hearts of thy people, and prepare their heart unto thee." Verses 16-18.

What do you suppose is the preparation of the heart of which David speaks? "And give unto Solomon my son a perfect heart, to keep thy commandments, thy testimonies, and thy statutes, and do all these things, and to build the palace for which I have made provision." Verse 19.

The heart must be prepared before the person can obey the law. The heart must be prepared before one steps through the door. A person must be as perfect as Christ's character can make him perfect. By faith the worshiper receives his righteousness from Christ. David said, "O Lord, emphasize on the minds of the people that their heart must contain the character of Christ before they move into the holy place." God never asks a person to obey the Ten Commandments until He first puts obedience into the life of that person. This is true in Old Testament times as well as in New.

ALMA: The heart spoken of here means the mind, doesn't it?

PASTOR LEWIS: That is right. A person has to prepare his mind to make this decision. This is exactly what David said. O God, prepare the people's mind to make that decision. And he says, Do it for my son Solomon that he might obey the law. This is important.

In Psalm 40:8 we find a prediction concerning Jesus Christ and in reality the experience of every true follower of the Lord. "I delight to do thy will, O my God: yea, thy law is within my heart." Notice David's response in verse 10: "I have not hid thy righteousness within my heart; I have declared thy faithfulness and thy salvation: I have not concealed thy lovingkindness and the truth from this great congregation."

Notice these two passages: "Thy righteousness within

41

my heart," and "thy law is in my heart." Obviously the word "law" and "righteousness" are synonymous. The thing that is important and that will lead us into this experience he said, "This righteousness that you gave me Lord, and put in my heart, I have not hid it. So obviously he obeyed it and exhibited it in his conduct. That is exactly what is going to result as we move into the sanctuary. It is important for us to see that once a person makes the decision "I will obey the law of God," and steps into the holy place he is obligated, as David said, to manifest that righteousness.

PASTOR BILL TUCKER: What is the priest's work? What is his function in the holy place?

PASTOR LEWIS: Now, that is a very pertinent question. The gold walls of the holy place represent the Ten Commandments. When an individual by faith endeavors to obey the law the record of his conduct comes up to heaven it will invariably show that his best obedience is contaminated with his own selfishness. Here is where the priest comes in. The priest brings in the blood of the sacrifice, puts blood on the horns of the altar of incense. This gives God the right to blot out that selfishness in the conduct of righteousness and He supplements His own perfect character to make up for the individual's faulty character.

In the court God gives the person perfection through Christ and in the most holy place He maintains that righteousness in the character of the individual. Now we will be better prepared to understand the deeper meaning of 1 John 1:9. "If we confess our sins, he is faithful and just to forgive us our sins, and to cleanse us from all unrighteousness."

When we confess, and that confession arises with the incense from the altar (representing the prayers of God's people), the priest will cleanse us from all unrighteousness. So what the priest is doing in the holy place is keeping the individual's record of conduct up to the high quality of obedience to the Ten Commandments. And so today, in the antitype, God is giving individuals perfection on the basis of their commitment, "By Your grace, Lord, I will obey."

PASTOR TUCKER: I surrender my life to whatever is His will.

PASTOR LEWIS: And He will supplement where you fall short.

PASTOR TUCKER: He supplies it **all** for us then.

PASTOR LEWIS: That is right. Now I would like to introduce you to a text which I consider one of the greatest in the entire Bible, not that I don't also have a great appreciation for John 3:16. It is 1 Kings 14:8. "And I have rent the kingdom away from the house of David, and give it to thee: and yet thou hast not been as my servant David, who kept my commandments, [from time to time], and who followed me with all of his heart [most of the time], who only did that which was right in mine eyes." How do you suppose the prophet could write so much about David, far more than other persons, and say he kept the commandments, followed God with **all** his heart, and did only that which was right in God's eyes? God supplemented David's character, and he needed supplementary work.

PASTOR TUCKER: Like when he saw the woman up there on the rooftop, and he had her husband slain.

PASTOR LEWIS: That is the part God had to wipe out with the blood of the altar, for David was coming short. But when he is judged in the light of the holy place, his life is considered as if it were right up to the top. Now, you see how the sanctuary is very appropriate.

PASTOR TUCKER: Let's think of a Christian. How does the Christian status differ in the holy place?

PASTOR LEWIS: Now you see, if a person, like the thief on the cross, made his committal to accept Christ (which he did) he stepped, as it were, into the holy place. So he was saved, and Christ gave him the assurance, "You will be there"—in the most holy place. In further answer to your question, let us notice Acts 26:18. "To open their eyes, and to turn them from darkness to light, and from the power of Satan unto God, that they may receive forgiveness of sins, and inheritance among them who are sanctified by faith that is in me."

Now you see, sanctification is an operation of what? Faith! You remember we mentioned the text that God has opened the door of faith to the Gentiles. Now He is opening to the Gentiles by faith the door of sanctification. This is character transformation.

In the ourter court there is forgiveness of sin. The outer door has been opened to you and to me and as we accept this salvation offered by Christ we have by faith instantaneous freedom from guilt of sin, through justification. By faith as we step through the door into the holy place there begins a repeated and continuing dedication of the mind and the life to the goal of perfection in Christ. This is a "work of a lifetime," climaxing in "an inheritance"—eternal life with God—the most holy place experience by faith in Christ.

Let's conclude with Hebrews 13:21, and note what God will do for every Christian who by faith moves through the sanctuary. "Now the God of peace, that brought again from the dead our Lord Jesus, that great shepherd of the sheep, through the blood of the everlasting covenant, make you perfect in every good work to do his will, working in you that which is wellpleasing in his sight, through Jesus Christ; to whom be glory forever and ever. Amen." If we follow through, God will make us perfect.

PASTOR TUCKER: Gorgeous. Thank you so much, Pastor

Lewis, for that wonderful inspiration. Haven't you been blessed today? And it all leads us to Jesus. He starts us on the way. He maintains us. And finally He will come and get us. Oh, we need to know that Man. He is called a man. He came and lived as a man. And He showed us how to live the victorious life.

A Man Named Jesus

I was young and full of life, living my own way
   I met a man who was walking on the King's Hiway,
He said, "Friend, please come walk with Me,
   By the way, my name is Jesus,"
I looked up in surprise and I said, "Oh Lord,
   What pleasure would be mine,
For I have so many things to do, maybe some other
   time."

Soon the years of time seemed to slip away
   My friends were all gone, living their own way,
I grew tired and I longed for a better day,
   Yes, I longed for the man named Jesus.

Then I asked everyone all along the way,
   "Do you know the Man, have you seen Him today?"
They just laughed with scorn, they had their games
   To play, they didn't know the Man named Jesus.

So then I walked along the crooked road of life one day,
   I met a Man who was walking on the narrow way,
He said, "Friend, please give your burden to Me,
   By the way, my name is Jesus."
I looked down with tear-dimmed eyes and I cried, "Oh
   Lord
   I was afraid we would never meet again."
He said, "I know, Oh how I know; but let's rejoice
   For I found you and saved you from sin."

So now we're walking hand in hand on the King's
    Hiway,
   And we're asking everyone "come and walk with us
     today."
Oh friend, don't you see, there's no other way,
   Come and walk with the Man named Jesus—Jesus.

Chapter 6
The Spiritual Meaning
of the
Furniture in the Holy Place

The three articles of furniture in the holy place of the sanctuary were: the seven golden candlesticks, the table of showbread, and the altar of incense. Each piece of furniture had a spiritual meaning.

The seven-branched golden candlestick was designated by God to be the light inside the building. "And thou shalt command the children of Israel, that they bring thee pure oil olive beaten for the light, to cause the lamp to burn always." Exodus 27:20. The lamps of the golden candlestick were fired by olive oil and burned night and day. The priests would put out three lamps, refurbish them, light them and then do the same to the other lamps. In this way the light never went out while the tabernacle was standing.

The golden candlestick had a very significant meaning as it pertained to Christ. "In him was life; and the life was the light of men." John 1:4. Here we see the Hebrew thinking displayed. Inasmuch as light was the means of their illumination, then this light became a symbol of the life of Christ. The beautiful transition is made—the light was the life of men. The seven-branched candlestick typified the light of the life of your Christian experience.

Jesus said, "I am the light of the world: he that followeth me shall not walk in darkness, but shall have the light of life." John 8:12. He was speaking of His life in the life of each one who follows Christ. Again we see how the Hebrew writers expressed truth in this way. "For thou wilt light my candle: the Lord my God will enlighten my darkness." Psalm 18:28.

The Hebrew way of expressing first the physical is followed by the spiritual interpretation. "You will light my candle." The physical feature is presented. Then David follows with the interpretation in the same verse by saying, "The Lord will enlighten my life." This is the same method we are presenting in the study of the sanctuary—the same method of interpretation. First we find the physical feature—the door, the altar, the court—then we look for the spiritual implication in the life of Christ and in our own personal lives.

The Table of Showbread

On the north side of the holy place (opposite the candlestick) was the table of showbread or the bread of His presence. The two stacks of six loaves of bread—twelve in all, representing the twelve tribes of Israel—were renewed every Sabbath day by the priests. This bread had a very significant meaning.

"For the bread of God is he which cometh down from heaven, and giveth life unto the world." John 6:33. We sometimes use the term "bread of life" meaning all food. Here again we see a very practical teaching medium. The priests would make the bread, place it on the table, eat the bread after renewing it the following Sabbath. As the priest ate this holy bread, it became a part of them.

This bread represented the body of Christ, and it became a part of their spiritual life.

"As the living Father had sent me, and I live by the Father: so he that eateth me, even he shall live by me." Verse 57. "Although He is God, yet while on earth in human flesh Jesus was completely dependent upon His Father." For every word He spoke and every deed He performed Christ was dependent upon His heavenly Father. "In this way the Christian is to be dependent upon Christ and to receive from Him the divine life and the divine nature. It is this eternal life that the Christian may partake of now, and is also this life that will bring him forth in the resurrection.." *Seventh-day Adventist Bible Commentary,* Volume 5, page 971.

"He that eateth me," must have been a shocking statement to Christ's listeners. However, they should have realized and we too, that to "eat" Jesus is to appropriate His life by faith. It is "to receive Him as our personal Saviour, believing that He forgives our sins, and that we are complete in Him." *The Desire of Ages,* page 389.

"It is not enough that we believe on Christ for the forgiveness of sin; we must by faith be constantly receiving spiritual strength and nourishment from him through his word. . . . 'The words that I speak unto you, they are spirit, and they are life.' (John 6:63). . . . The followers of Christ must be partakers of his experience. They must receive and assimilate the word of God so that it shall become the motive power of life and action. By the power of Christ they must be changed into his likeness, and reflect the divine attributes." *Patriarchs and Prophets,* by Ellen G. White, pages 277, 278.

Altar of Incense

The altar of incense was placed beside the veil which separated the holy place from the most holy place. (See

Exodus 30:1-6.) The sanctuary had a gabled roof and the veil only reached to the beginning of the gable, allowing plenty of room above the veil for the burned incense to ascend, go over the veil into the area which represented heaven itself—the most holy place. When the priest offered incense before the Lord, he looked toward the ark of the covenant on the other side of the veil in the most holy place. As the cloud of incense arose, the divine glory descended upon the mercy-seat and filled the most holy place.

The incense ascending into the most holy place represented the merits and intercession of Christ, His perfect righteousness, which through faith was imputed to His people. The time of the morning and evening sacrifice in the outer court was also the time of the incense in the holy place. This was a time of intense interest to the worshipers who assembled at the tabernacle. Before entering into the presence of God through the ministration of the priest, they were to engage in earnest searching of heart and confession of sin. They united in silent prayer, with their faces toward the holy place. In this way their petitions ascended with the cloud of incense, while faith laid hold upon the merits of the promised Saviour prefigured by the atoning sacrifice on the altar of burnt offering in the court.

As the priest looked by faith to the mercy-seat which he could not see, so the people of God today are to direct their prayers to Christ, their great high priest, who, unseen by human vision, is pleading in our behalf in the heavenly sanctuary above.

The psalmist well understood the deep meaning of the altar of incense when he wrote, "Let my prayer be set forth before thee as incense; and the lifting up of my heart as the evening sacrifice." Psalm 141:2. Incense was added each morning to the altar of incense and again in the evening to encourage morning and evening prayer by the congregation. Since the flame was burning continually on the altar of incense, the lesson was taught that the worshiper should continually live in the attitude of prayer and supplication. It was also good to know that Christ was continually interceding in man's behalf. "I pray for them: I pray not for the world, but for them which thou hast given me; for they are thine." John 17:9.

In Christ's life and continuing ministry in behalf of His people the purpose of the altar of incense is fulfilled. We have observed that every piece of furniture in the holy place pointed the worshiper to the coming Messiah and what He would do for His people. He would be the Light of the world and through Him His people would be the light of the world. "Let your light so shine before men that they may see your good works."

"I am the Bread of Life." God has given the bread of life to us that we might break it to the world. And the incense ascending from the altar of incense represented the merits and intercession of Christ, so we are to be a sweet incense to our family, neighbors, and friends, interceding for them and pointing them to the saving merits of our lovely Saviour.

The Holy Spirit and the Holy Place

Inasmuch as the court around the sanctuary speaks to us of Calvary—the altar of burnt offering—and the water of life—the laver—we might say that the court represents Christ. The holy place refers to the person and deity of the Holy Spirit. The most holy place refers to the Father. So the three apartments are applicable to the three persons of the Deity.

In the holy place there is oil in the seven-branched candlestick. There is oil in the bread and oil mixed with the incense. Oil is a symbol of the Holy Spirit. So we can see how the holy place could rightly represent the Holy

Spirit

The three pieces of furniture in the holy place of the sanctuary reveal three ways in which Christ is manifested to us. Also it reveals three ways in which the individual may increase his life in Christ. He must have the light of Christ's life. He must have the food which is the inspired word—the Holy Bible. He must constantly read it and eat it until it becomes a part of his life. He must through daily prayer maintain contact with heaven. And the power of the Holy Spirit enables him to accomplish all this.

The apostle Paul expressed this experience in these words: "I am crucified with Christ: nevertheless I live; yet not I, but Christ liveth in me: and the life which I now live in the flesh I live by the faith of the Son of God, who loved me, and gave himself for me." Galatians 2:20.

As the priest stood in the holy place before the eternal law of God, representing the congregation, the actual presence of God was surrounding him. Wherever he looked within the holy place he saw furniture that represented Jesus and he knew that oil of the lamps, the oil in the bread, and the oil in the incense represented the Holy Spirit. Now the priest realized that there was only one way that he could live up to that high standard of godly righteousness—the Ten Commandment law— a transcript of the character of God. He could accomplish this only through Christ, the coming Redeemer and Saviour. This was the deep meaning that the priest was to teach the congregation. This is what the priest was to spend his time doing when he was not serving in the sanctuary—teaching the people the way of salvation. And the apostle Paul revealed this great truth to us so clearly. The only way we can keep God's eternal law, His Ten Commandments, is to allow Christ by the Holy Spirit to live out His obedient life within us moment by moment of every day.

"The law of ten commandments is not to be looked upon as much from the prohibitory side, as from the mercy side. Its prohibitions are the sure guarantee of happiness in obedience. As received in Christ, it works in us the purity of character that will bring joy to us through eternal ages. To the obedient it is a wall of protection." Ellen G. White, *Selected Messages,* Volume 1, page 235.

The purpose of the Ten Commandments is to be a wall of protection. This is the lesson of the gold wall in the sanctuary. The gold wall went completely around the tabernacle—both the holy place and the most holy place. Its purpose was to protect the individual from being destroyed by sin. Jesus said, "He that hath my commandments, and keepeth them, he it is that loveth me: and he that loveth me shall be loved of my Father, and I will love him, and will manifest myself to him." John 14:21.

What a paradox: If we keep God's commandments Christ will manifest Himself to us and only as He manifests Himself to us are we enabled to keep His commandments. This is what the sanctuary has taught us. This is the teaching of Jesus. This is the relationship of law and the gospel. Only as Christ lives out His obedient life in us are we enabled to keep God's commandments. And Jesus said, "Ye are my friends, if ye do whatsoever I command you." John 15:14.

Are you His friend? Have you developed that beautiful relationship with Him by daily feasting on the "Bread of Life"? Are you allowing the "Light of the world" to shine through you daily? Are you continually in the attitude of prayer that Christ's merits and intercession, His perfect righteousness by faith is being imputed to you daily? If not, begin to build that relationship today.

Accept Him as your Saviour now. Commit your life to Him. Tell Him, "Whatever You want me to do, by Your grace I will do it. I want to be Your friend."

I'll Be a Friend of His

When I think how Jesus suffered on the cross for me
Dying there in shame and agony
So that I could be redeemed and live eternally,
I can do no less than now exclaim:

"I'll be a friend of His through all my days!
I'll walk life's road with Him and sing His praise!
Tho others pass Him by and walk away,
I'll be a friend of His—His will obey!
I never could repay the debt I owe
For all He's done for me—full well I know;
But I can live for Him who died for me,
And be a friend of His for eternity!

Some day in the glory I shall see Him face to face
There I'll fall before His nail-pierced feet,
Thank Him for His mercy and redeeming love and
    grace,
His sweet name adoring repeat.

I'll be a friend of His through all my days!
I'll walk life's road with Him and sing His praise!
Tho others pass Him by and walk away,
I'll be a friend of His—His will obey!
I never could repay the debt I owe
For all He's done for me—full well I know;
But I can live for Him who died for me,
And be a friend of His for eternity!

Chapter 7
Walls of Salvation

There are two distinctive walls in the sanctuary: the white linen wall around the court and the gold wall around the tabernacle proper. "In that day shall this song be sung in the land of Judah; We have a strong city; salvation will God appoint for walls and bulwarks." Isaiah 26:1.

God has appointed the walls for a bulwark. To gain a proper understanding of the sanctuary one must clearly grasp the meaning of the many symbols used. One way to understand the symbol is to physically analyze that symbol. In this case we are considering the walls—a wall of white linen and a wall that is gold.

To interpret this symbol properly a person should ask: Why is the wall around the outside? It was about 14 feet high and the gold wall was much higher and could be seen above the outer wall. Walls are generally for protection. Walls of a house, a fence around a field, and especially walls around a city are for protection. This is precisely the purpose of these walls.

There are two distinctive aspects of protection that will be involved in these walls. The Bible text suggested that they are appointed for bulwarks to protect the person from certain violence, certain intrusions, certain situations which might cause hurt. In the fifth chapter of Isaiah the prophet speaks of walls as a protection around Jerusalem.

"Now will I sing to my well-beloved a song of my beloved touching his vineyard. My well-beloved hath a vineyard in a very fruitful hill: And he fenced it, and gathered out the stones thereof, and planted it with the choicest vine, and built a tower in the midst of it, and also made a winepress therein: and he looked that it should bring forth grapes, and it brought forth wild grapes. . . . And now go to; I will tell you what I will do to my vineyard: I will take away the hedge thereof, and it shall be eaten up; and break down the wall thereof, and it shall be trodden down." Isaiah 5:1-5.

The hedge—the wall—symbolizes protection. In verse 7 Isaiah explains the meaning of the vineyard. "The vineyard of the Lord of hosts is the house of Israel." So he is talking about a vineyard in the sense of vines, and he is also talking about the vineyard representing the people of Israel. First he presents the literal or physical and then he makes the spiritual application. God has built a hedge or a fence around His people.

Now let's get back to the sanctuary. In Exodus 38:16 we are told: "All the hangings of the court round about were of fine twined linen." The outer wall was made of fine twined linen. That wall was about 100 feet long and 50 feet wide. Let us first consider how the white outer wall applies to salvation and we will see it differs from the gold wall.

"And it came to pass, when Moses had made an end of writing the words of this law in a book, until they were finished, That Moses commanded the Levites, which bare the ark of the covenant of the Lord, saying, Take this book of the law, and put it in the side of the ark of the covenant of the Lord your God, that it may be a witness against thee." Deuteronomy 31:24-26.

The law of Moses—having to do with the burnt offerings, sacrifices, meat offerings, sin offerings, and all the various ordinances concerning the sanctuary—was written by Moses in a book and placed, not inside the ark of the covenant, but on the outside of the ark. However, the Ten Commandment law was written by God on tables of stone and placed inside the ark of the covenant. "And the Lord said unto Moses, Come up to me into the mount, and be there: and I will give thee tables of stone, and a law, and commandments which I have written; that thou mayest teach them." Exodus 24:12. "And he gave unto Moses, when he had made an end of communing with him upon mount Sinai, two tables of testimony, tables of stone, written with the finger of God." Exodus 31:18. "And he took and put the testimony into the ark." Exodus 40:20.

So there are the ceremonial laws or the law of Moses, and the moral law, the law of God—the Ten Commandments. The white wall surrounded the court where the children of Israel offered the sacrifices on the altar of burnt offering. It is the sacrificial system that is described in the ceremonial law—the law of Moses. It was not described in the Ten Commandment law.

The law of Moses pointed out that if a man sinned he was to show a repentant spirit by bringing a lamb into the court and killing the lamb on the north side of the altar, confessing his sin to God. And as the sinner looked around he saw the white wall. Though his sin may have been of scarlet hue, now by faith in the coming Saviour his sins have been made "white as snow." He is justified by faith. That is what this white wall says—Justified!

When Paul reached Rome he soon asked to talk with the leaders of the Jews. "And when they had appointed him a day, there came many to him into his lodging; to whom he expounded and testified the kingdom of God, persuading them concerning Jesus, both out of the law of Moses, and out of the prophets, from morning till evening." Acts 28:23. Out of the law of Moses, Paul reasoned with the Jewish leaders in Rome about the lamb representing Christ, about the lamb being killed and how that was fulfilled on Calvary. He explained how Christ's life was sacrificed to pay the penalty for sin.

Now in the Ten Commandments there are no instructions about salvation, once a person has violated that law. There is no salvation from sin in the Ten Commandments. There is penalty for sin in the Ten Commandments, but no salvation. That is the necessity for the ceremonial laws, represented by the white wall, to reveal what God would do to take away sin. God would actually allow His Son to come and die to pay the penalty for sin. So the white wall, representing the ceremonial laws written by Moses in a book, revealed to the repentant sinner how God would deal with sin and how he could have salvation through faith in the coming Messiah.

Many months after Paul's first visit with the Jewish leaders in Rome he wrote a letter to them and the young Christian church. "For all have sinned, and come short of the glory of God; Being justified freely by his grace through the redemption that is in Christ Jesus; . . . That he (God) might be just, and the justifier of him which believeth in Jesus. Where is boasting then? It is excluded. By what law? of works? Nay: but by the law of faith." Romans 3:23-27. Paul excludes this aspect of works which would be represented by the gold wall. It has to be the law of faith. The sinner must look to the works of Christ and by faith accept His works in order to move on in his Christian experience into the holy place.

In a previous study we read about the "door of faith." Acts 14:27. Now we are learning about the wall of faith. One great truth we are learning in our study of the sanctuary is this: The purpose of all of the sacrifices was to demonstrate the repentant sinner's faith in a coming Saviour. The only way into the sanctuary was through the door of faith, connected to the wall of faith. A person must come in by believing in Christ as his personal Saviour. Once he does, he is in the area where the atonement will take place and Christ will die for his sins. His sins will be placed on the altar so he can enjoy the freedom from the ills of sin. This wall is protecting him from the ill conduct of his former life. If he were left to himself, he would finally be destroyed. So a repentant sinner finds salvation solely by faith in the coming Redeemer who would die for his sins providing him with complete justification—perfect righteousness.

"What shall we say then? That the Gentiles, which followed not after righteousness, have attained to righteousness, even the righteousness which is of faith." Romans 9:30. "The righteousness which is of faith." There is that white wall again. Why not some other color? Because white is a symbol of justification.

As you look at the sanctuary walls you might ask, "What is the difference between the white wall and the gold wall?" In the white wall it is the works of another Person given to us to justify us. Immediately upon being justified his life is righteous. His life is in harmony with the Ten Commandments—the gold wall. But the person who gets this righteousness did not do the living of it. Christ did the living of it and transfers it to him by faith. That is why the wall is white.

With this relationship with Christ a person saved by grace now steps through the doorway into the holy place. With only the righteousness of Christ in his life what will he seek to do? We can find the answer in Luke 6:45. "A good man out of the good treasure of his heart bringeth forth that which is good; and an evil man out of the evil treasure of his heart bringeth forth that which is evil: for of the abundance of the heart his mouth speaketh."

Here we find the word "good" mentioned three times. First we need to clearly understand how this good man got a good heart. Christ gave him the good heart by putting the law of God in his heart. Then out of that good heart comes forth good—good words, good works. But the good that this person has is not of his own works. It was what Christ gave him. He said, "I will put my law in their inward parts, and write it in their hearts; and will be their God, and they shall be my people." Jeremiah 31:33. So when God puts the good or the law or the love in the heart or mind of the individual, now he can begin to bring out of that mind the goodness that God has given him.

"And the law is not of faith: but, The man that doeth them shall live in them." Galatians 3:12. This particular law or wall is based upon works. This wall or law is not of faith. We have already shown very distinctly that the law of Moses was of faith—the white wall. But the Ten Commandment law—God's moral law—is not of faith, but of works. In order for the person to be in a position to move into the area of the protection of the gold wall he would have to have the character of that wall in his life. But he himself cannot produce it. He must pick it up as a free gift from Christ—justification! Now he is able to move into the holy place and the gold wall will afford a tremendous protection for him.

Let us notice the wonderful relationship of the gold wall to the white wall. "Do we then make void the law through faith? God forbid: yea, we establish the law." Romans 3:31. Does the gold wall work contrary to the white wall? Is one contrary to the other? Is faith antagonistic to law or is grace and law a supplement to each other? an aid to each other?

Christ lived the righteousness of the law day by day. He said, "I have kept my Father's commandments."

John 15:10. IT IS THIS RIGHTEOUSNESS HE GIVES TO US. Once He gives it to us and we move into the holy place in our daily living, does the righteousness that Christ gave us to aid us to live victoriously each day destroy this gold wall? NO! Paul says, "God forbid." Salvation by grace through faith in Jesus Christ does not destroy the law but establishes it more firmly. The gold wall is more sturdy and much stronger. And now we begin to assimilate that law—the righteousness of Christ—into our own characters, which otherwise could not be accomplished. And sanctification—the work of a lifetime—begins.

Now you see why I could say geographically you have to come in this door, behind this wall of faith. Then you must move from this door into the aspect of good works—sanctification. But you can only accomplish this through Christ. You have no ability to obey the law of God. But Christ has made it possible. He says, "Through my personal representative I will come and live my obedient life within you, if you will only surrender yourself to me." (Galatians 2:20.) The response to this invitation is of utmost importance, for everything depends on the right action of your will. You cannot change your heart but you can choose to serve God. Jesus said, "If you love me, keep my commandments." John 14:15. You can make the choice. "I choose to obey Him, because I love Him so much for living and dying for me." Through this decision of your will an entire change can be made in your life. "By yielding up your will to Christ, you ally yourself with the power that is above all principalities and powers. You will have strength from above to hold you steadfast, and thus through constant surrender to God, you will be enabled to live the new life, even the life of faith." Ellen G. White, *Steps to Christ,* page 48. This is when steady growth in sanctification takes place through Christ.

Now let's look at this beautiful truth in the light of the sanctuary. As I come to the entrance of the sanctuary I see in the door a deep meaning. There is revealed the righteous character of Christ. Also I see clearly revealed His shed blood for me. His grace alone begins to quicken the lifeless faculties of my soul and I am drawn to God. I long for a pure and holy life. I make the choice to go through that door—I accept Christ as the door; I accept Him as my personal Saviour because I love Him for what He has done for me. Instantly He gives me a righteous life according to the law of God—which is the love of God. Now what must I do with that love since it is in my life? My will must choose to manifest that love that Christ gave me. Gradually but surely I begin to exhibit this wall—the gold wall—in my daily life. And the moment Christ begins to live out His obedient life in me this gold wall—the law of God—begins to construct around me. This wall—the righteous character of Christ—is the strength of my life. It is my protector, my bulwark against temptation and sin. Day by day that righteous character of Christ becomes firmly established in and around my life.

The difference between the white and the gold wall in my life and yours is this: Christ gave you the white wall as a gift from His life. However, it becomes gold when you put it into your conduct. It is love in action. Pure gold. There is only one place it fits in your life and that is in your conduct. You can't take Christ's character or life and say, I'm going to wear it around my neck or around my arm, or I'll put it in my pocket, or in my Bible. There is only one place—He must be seen in my life, in your life. That's why He said, "If you love me, keep my commandments."

Like Jesus

Teach me Father, what to say;
Teach me Father, how to pray;
Teach me all along the way,
How to be like Jesus.

I would be like Jesus,
I would be like Jesus,
Help me, Lord, to daily grow
More and more like Jesus.

Teach me that the time is short,
Teach me how to live and work,
Teach me that to never shirk
Is to be like Jesus.

I would be like Jesus,
I would be like Jesus,
Help me Lord, to daily grow
More and more like Jesus.

Teach me how we may be one,
Like the Father and the Son;
And when all is overcome,
I would be like Jesus.

I would be like Jesus,
I would be like Jesus,
Help me Lord, to daily grow
More and more like Jesus.

Chapter 8
Into the Holiest Place

The question before us today is: How does the believer move on into the sanctuary? From what we have discussed before one would suspect that the priest must lead the way.

"Wherefore, holy brethren, partakers of the heavenly calling, consider the Apostle and High Priest of our profession, Christ Jesus." Hebrews 3:1. The perfect character of Christ's humanity, attached to His priesthood and His deity are the factors that are going to lead the way back to the throne of God.

"Let us therefore come boldly unto the throne of grace, that we may obtain mercy, and find grace to help in time of need." Hebrews 4:16. We are encouraged to come boldly into the most holy place. How can this be accomplished? Since Christ took His humanity that He got from His earthly mother into the heavenly sanctuary, it is going to be contingent upon the believer to lay hold on His humanity and follow Him in. But there is a quality of life that must be obtained.

There is a tragic story told in the tenth chapter of Leviticus about Nadab and Abihu, the sons of Aaron. In a drunken stupor these priests took their censers and put fire in them that God had not kindled, and put incense on the coals, "and offered strange fire before the Lord. . . . And there went out fire from the Lord, and devoured them, and they died before the Lord. Then Moses said unto Aaron, This is it that the Lord spake, saying, I will be sanctified in them that come nigh me, and before all the people I will be glorified. And Aaron held his peace." Leviticus 10:1-3.

Nadab and Abihu approached God in a way that was improper. This scripture makes it plain that anyone who comes into God's presence must be holy. And yet, who of us would say that we are holy? How can we be invited to "come boldly" into God's presence? "We have not an high priest which cannot be touched with the feeling of our infirmities; but was in all points tempted like as we are, yet without sin. Let us therefore come boldly unto the throne of grace." Hebrews 4:15, 16. We have a High Priest—Jesus Christ—100% human and yet 100% divine. He lived as a man without sinning. Only as we attach ourselves to Christ's humanity, which He made holy by His obedience to God, can we approach God with boldness.

God's throne is depicted in the most holy place by the ark of the covenant, which encloses the Ten Commandment law, written with the finger of God, and the mercy seat—the lid which covered the ark. God is holy and anyone who is going to approach that throne must have the basic quality of God's character—holiness.

The 53rd chapter of Isaiah refers to Christ's preparation and His work to get us into the actual presence of God. "He was oppressed, and he was afflicted, yet he opened not his mouth: he is brought as a lamb to the slaughter, and as a sheep before her shearers is dumb, so he opened not his mouth." Isaiah 53:7. Here Christ is referred to as the "lamb." From the gates of the Garden of Eden and all through the Old Testament lambs had been used to represent and point forward to Christ. Finally John the Baptist said prior to Christ's baptism, "Behold the lamb of God."

"He was taken from prison and from judgment: and who shall declare his generation? for he was cut off out of the land of the living: for the transgression of my people was he stricken." Verse 8. Here is revealed that by divine power and ability lying in the capacity of deity, God was going to take the sins of the human race on His person. What a tremendous transfer! Here is the basic concept of the plan of salvation!

"And he made his grave with the wicked, and with the rich in his death." Verse 9. The Hebrew word for "death" is the plural form. This indicates that the Messiah is going to die more than one death. He is going to have to save the whole human race. So his death is going to go beyond the capacity of one human being. He will die not only the first death but also the second death—the death for the whole human race.

"Yet it pleased the Lord to bruise him; he hath put him to grief: when thou shalt make his soul an offering for sin, he shall see his seed, he shall prolong his days, and the pleasure of the Lord shall prosper in his hand." Verse 10. Here is the basic issue in the whole sanctuary revelation. We have been talking about sacrifices, lambs, opening doors and going through doors. We have been talking about furniture and walls. But now we have come to the great issue. He gave His soul as a sacrifice for sin.

From a Biblical background you recognize that the word "soul," "*nephesh*" in Hebrew, is the word for mind. Christ gave His mind a sacrifice for sin. The writer of the book of Hebrews said, "For it is not possible that the blood of bulls and of goats should take away sins." Hebrews 10:4. That is true. They could only represent symbolically what Christ was to do. But now we have come to the real issue. In Christ's mind He is going to go through an experience that fulfills all the sacrifices that have ever been made from the gates of Eden. This is very important for us and gives us a tremendous appreciation of what Christ did to save us.

"For even hereunto were ye called: because Christ also suffered for us, leaving us an example, that ye should follow his steps: Who did no sin, neither was guile found in his mouth: Who, when he was reviled, reviled not again; when he suffered, he threatened not. . . . Who his own self bare our sins in his own body on the tree, that we, being dead to sins, should live unto righteousness: by whose stripes ye were healed." 1 Peter 2:21-24.

Do we get a deeper appreciation of what Christ did with our sins? He took those sins into His mind. He took them into His conscious intelligence. He didn't just write them on a piece of paper and put them in His pocket or put them down on a record book in heaven. NO! He took them where they were going to kill Him.

Now the people who die of this world who do not lay hold upon the plan of salvation are going to have to die the second death described in Revelation 20. In their mind is where the suffering and the death will take place. That is why Jesus must suffer this kind of death, making it possible that you will never have to experience it.

It almost seems blasphemous to say this but we must get right to the point. We must approach it very cautiously, yet make it plain. Christ took my sin. That means if you are a liar, Christ felt as if He were a liar. If you are an adulterer, Christ felt that He was an adulterer in His conscious mind. If He takes these sins into His conscious mind, what is that going to do to Him? The scripture plainly says, "Your iniquities have separated between you and your God." Isaiah 59:2. Christ is conscious of guilt and sin, yet He did no sin; but He is made sin for us (2 Corinthians 5:21). In His mind the oneness that He has had with the Father is beginning to break up. He seems to be getting farther and farther separated. To Him it seems like an eternal separation. And He cries out, "Eli, Eli, lama sabachthani!" "My God, why have You left me." "He feared that sin was so offensive to God, that their separation was to be eternal." *The Desire of Ages,* page 753.

The night before in the Garden of Gethsemane is when this separating experience began. As Christ fell prostrate upon the ground in Gethsemane, "He felt that by sin He was being separated from His Father. The gulf was so broad, so black, so deep, that His spirit shuddered before it. This agony He must not exert His divine power to escape. As man He must suffer the consequences of man's sin. As man He must endure the wrath of God against transgression." *Ibid.,* page 686. Little by little the Holy Spirit is being squeezed out of His life. As the sins and guilt of the world are placed upon Christ the Holy Spirit is squeezed from His life. He could not have a realization of separation from God if He still had the Holy Spirit in His life. Gethsemane in Hebrew means "to crush out the oil." So the Holy Spirit is crushed out of His life. Now He is in the capacity of a man—a sinful man—and without the Holy Spirit.

The agony of the night and the next day continue. In His mind, Christ is under the pressure of the world's sins. In His body He endures the beating, the pulling out of His beard hair by hair, spit in His face, anything and everything to get Him to express audibly these sins in His conscious mind. But not one word came from His lips. When He was reviled He did not retaliate. He opened not His mouth to let those sins of the human race get out into expression. Everytime He did speak it revealed the character of God.

As the darkness and gloom lifted from the cross, in clear, trumpet-like tones Jesus cried, "It is finished." "Amid the awful darkness, apparently forsaken of God, Christ had drained the last dregs in the cup of human woe. In those dreadful hours He had relied upon the evidence of His Father's acceptance heretofore given Him. . . . By faith He rested in His Father's justice, mercy and great love. In faith and total submission, He speaks once more: 'Father, into Thy hands I commend My spirit.' A light encircled the cross, and the face of the Saviour shone with a glory like the sun. He then bowed His head and died. By faith, Christ was victor." *Ibid.*, page 756.

When Christ died on the cross of Calvary something most unusual happened in the sanctuary—in the temple in Jerusalem. "Jesus, when he had cried again with a loud voice, yielded up the ghost. And, behold, the veil of the temple was rent in twain from the top to the bottom; and the earth did quake, and the rocks rent." Matthew 27:50, 51. It was the veil between the holy place and the most holy place that was torn from the top to the bottom. God's law, written with His own finger, had once been in that most holy place. If a person transgressed—sinned against God, broke the law of God—the penalty was death. But Christ had now paid the penalty and the veil was miraculously torn from top to bottom so there was nothing to separate the two compartments.

In reality it was Christ's suffering and eternal death for the human race that opened the door into the most holy place. "Having therefore, brethren, boldness to enter into the holiest by the blood of Jesus, By a new and living way, which he hath consecrated for us, through the veil, that is to say, his flesh." Hebrews 10:19, 20. This blood of Jesus is His sufferings on Calvary that ended in eternal death. So it is because of

His blood that we now have boldness to enter into the most holy place. But it should never be forgotten that without His living a sinless life in complete obedience to the will of God, His blood would have been to no avail. So it is His righteous life and His blood that makes it possible for me to enter into the holiest.

"The great sacrifice has been made. The way into the holiest is laid open. A new and living way is prepared for all. No longer need sinful, sorrowing humanity await the coming of [some earthly] high priest. From this moment on the Saviour was to officiate as priest and advocate in the heaven of heavens. It was as if a living voice had spoken to the worshipers: There is now an end to all sacrifices and offerings for sin. The Son of God is come according to His word, 'Lo, I come (in the volume of the book it is written of Me,) to do Thy will, O God.' 'By His own blood' He entereth 'in once into the holy place, having obtained eternal redemption for us.'" *Ibid.*, page 757.

The victorious life of Christ is our sanctification. At every stage in Christ's growth, from childhood to the cross, His life was perfect. Though tempted and harassed by the enemy every step of the way, yet Christ as a man lived a sinless life. Now He has opened the new and living way for everyone to live this victorious life. "At every stage of development our life may be perfect; yet if God's purpose for us is fulfilled, there will be continual advancement. Sanctification is the work of a lifetime." *Christ's Object Lessons*, page 65. In the most holy place our High Priest today is effecting transformations, perfecting a people to live with Him throughout all eternity. Even the enemy is completely mystified by the mighty transforming power of God in the lives of Christ's yielded followers.

"Rejoice not against me, O mine enemy: when I fall, I shall arise; when I sit in darkness, the Lord shall be a light unto me. I will bear the indignation of the Lord, because I have sinned against him, until he plead my cause, and execute judgment for me: he will bring me forth to the light, and I shall behold his righteousness." Micah 7:8, 9. So Christ is my sanctification. I am going in on His merits—His humanity—which I claim as my righteousness. So when He brings me into judgment, God says, "I will behold His righteousness."

"Who is a God like unto thee, that pardoneth iniquity, and passeth by the transgression of the remnant of his heritage? he retaineth not his anger for ever, because he delighteth in mercy." Micah 7:18. "He passes over" is the meaning of the mercy seat—the lid to the ark of the covenant, wherein lies the Ten Commandments. By putting the blood on the mercy seat, God passes over their sins.

"He will turn again, he will have compassion upon us; he will subdue our iniquities; and thou wilt cast all their sins into the depths of the sea." Verse 19. He has subdued our sins with His life and His death. And here at the mercy seat is where the application is made. It was on Calvary where the blood was shed. But it is in heaven—in the throne room, at the mercy seat—where our High Priest, our precious Saviour applies the blood. And if He has applied it for you, you have everlasting life.

Only Jesus Can Satisfy Your Soul

The world will try to satisfy that longing in your soul.
You may search the wide world o'er but you'll be just as
    before.
You'll never find true satisfaction until you've found
    the Lord,
For only Jesus can satisfy your soul.

Only Jesus can satisfy your soul;
And only He can change your heart and make you
    whole.
He'll give you peace you never knew,
Sweet love and joy, and heaven too;
For only Jesus can satisfy your soul!

If you could have the fame and fortune, all the wealth
    you could obtain,
Yet you have not Christ within, your living here would
    be in vain.
There'll come a time when death shall call you, riches
    cannot help you then,
So come to Jesus for only He can satisfy.

Only Jesus can satisfy your soul;
And only He can change your heart and make you
    whole.
He'll give you peace you never knew,
Sweet love and joy, and heaven too;
For only Jesus can satisfy your soul!

Chapter 9
Blood on the Altars

Often the question is asked, Why did God require so much blood in Old Testament times? Blood on the altars! Blood on the mercy seat of the ark! Why all the blood!

It must ever be kept in mind that the shedding of blood was not God's original plan for man or beast. But because of sin, because of negligence of man in obeying God, another plan was instituted which involved the shedding of blood of goats, lambs, and rams.

There is an experience in the life of David that helps us to better understand why the blood on the altars. It would be well to read the entire 24th chapter of Second Samuel. But because of time and space we will read only a few passages. Because David sinned in numbering Israel, the Lord allowed the people to be smitten with pestilence and seventy thousand men died. Then David repented of his sin. "And David's heart smote him after that he had numbered the people. And David said unto the Lord, I have sinned greatly in that I have done: and now, I beseech thee, O Lord, take away the iniquity of thy servant; for I have done very foolishly." 2 Samuel 24:10.

King David was specific in his prayer. "I have sinned."

"Take away the iniquity of thy servant." He recognized his sin and was anxious that it be removed. David was instructed to go to the threshingfloor of Araunah and build an altar unto the Lord. "And Araunah said, Wherefore is my lord the king come to his servant? And David said, to buy the threshingfloor of thee, to build an altar unto the Lord, that the plague may be stayed from the people." Verse 21.

Araunah offered the threshingfloor and the oxen for sacrifice as a gift. But "the king said unto Araunah, Nay; but I will surely buy it of thee at a price: neither will I offer burnt offerings unto the Lord my God of that which doth cost me nothing. So David bought the threshingfloor and the oxen for fifty sheckels of silver. And David built there an altar unto the Lord, and offered burnt offerings and peace offerings. So the Lord was intreated for the land, and the plague was stayed from Israel." Verses 24 and 25.

The place where David built his altar was the very same place that Abraham had built an altar to offer Isaac as a sacrifice. Later Solomon built the temple on this very site.

By David's act of repentance for his sin of numbering Israel and building an altar to the Lord and offering sacrifices, the "Lord was intreated" and the plague was stopped.

In that marvelous book, *The Great Controversy Between Christ and Satan,* written by Ellen G. White, on page 629 we find this statement: "The pleading blood of Christ has shielded the sinner from receiving the full measure of his guilt." When a person by faith offered his sacrifice and the blood was placed on the altar, the guilt was transferred to Christ. God, in His mercy, does not permit all the consequences of one's transgressions to come upon the one who sinned. Christ shields the sinner from receiving the full measure of his guilt. This shows the attitude of God toward the sinner. He willingly takes the punishment for sin upon Himself.

Not only was the blood of the sacrifice placed upon the altar of sacrifice in the court but it was also brought into the holy place and put on the altar of incense. "If the priest that is anointed do sin according to the sin of the people; then let him bring for his sin, which he hath sinned, a young bullock without blemish unto the Lord for a sin offering. And he shall bring the bullock unto the door of the tabernacle of the congregation before the Lord; and shall lay his hand upon the bullock's head, and kill the bullock before the Lord. And the priest that is anointed shall take of the bullock's blood, and bring it to the tabernacle of the congregation; And the priest shall dip his finger in the blood, and sprinkle of the blood seven times before the Lord, before the veil of the sanctuary. And the priest shall put some of the blood upon the horns of the altar of sweet incense before the Lord, which is in the tabernacle of the congregation." Leviticus 4:3-7.

When the priest sinned or when the whole congregation of Israel sinned this procedure was followed: "And if the whole congregation of Israel sin through ignorance, and the thing be hid from the eyes of the assembly, and they have done somewhat against any of the commandments of the Lord concerning things which should not be done, and are guilty; When the sin, which they have sinned against it is known, then the congregations shall offer a young bullock for the sin, and bring him before the tabernacle of the congregation. And the elders of the congregation shall lay their hands upon the head of the bullock before the Lord: and the bullock shall be killed before the Lord. And the priest that is anointed shall bring of the bullock's blood to the tabernacle of the congregation: And the priest shall dip his finger in some of the blood, and sprinkle it seven times before the Lord, even before the veil." Leviticus 4:13-17.

The anointed priest—the high priest—stood for and represented the people. The high priest, being in a special sense a figure of Christ, was the representative man. He stood for all Israel. He carried their burdens and sins. When he sinned, Israel sinned. When he entered the sanctuary, he went in on behalf of the people. And when he appeared before God, they appeared.

When an individual sinned and he repented of that sin and brought a sacrificial lamb, the blood of that lamb was placed only on the horns of the altar of sacrifice in the court. But when the anointed or high priest sinned or the congregation sinned and repentance shown, the bullock was sacrificed. The blood was brought into the holy place and sprinkled before the veil—before the law of God—and the blood was also placed on the horns of the altar of incense.

It is of utmost importance that the blood is not only *shed*, for atonement is made for the sin only when the blood is *applied*. And when the blood was applied to the horns of the altar it meant that God was covering His people—their sins were forgiven.

When Balaam was asked to curse the children of Israel, the Lord met Balaam and put words in his mouth. One of the things that God told Balaam to say was this: "He hath not beheld iniquity in Jacob, neither hath he seen perverseness in Israel." Numbers 23:21. Can you imagine God saying such a thing? "No iniquity in Jacob and no sin in Israel." Certainly to make that observation is very gracious on God's part. How could He do that? Because of the blood that was placed on the horns of the altar of incense which covered the sins of the people. You can see how merciful God is. So here we have pictured the righteousness of Christ covering the confessed sins of the people. The blood sprinkled and applied took away the transgression of the anointed priest or the whole congregation and established them with the righteousness of Christ's character, typified by the gold wall of the holy place which represented the Ten Commandments.

Here is revealed justification and sanctification side by side. The white wall around the court symbolized justification provided by the death of Christ. In the tabernacle itself—the holy place and the most holy place, with the Ten Commandments in the ark of the covenant—the gold wall symbolized sanctification provided by the righteous character of Christ.

There is another question that needs to be answered: "Why was the blood placed on the mercy seat of the ark of the covenant in the most holy place?" "Why would the blood finally come to this particular position in the sanctuary behind the last veil in the most holy place?" Let us turn to the book of Leviticus containing a tremendous revelation regarding the blood in the last area. "And he shall take the two goats, and present them before the Lord at the door of the tabernacle of the congregation. And Aaron shall cast lots upon the two goats; one lot for the Lord, and the other lot for the scapegoat. And Aaron shall bring the goat upon which the Lord's lot fell, and offer him for a sin offering. But the goat, on which the lot fell to be the scapegoat, shall be presented alive before the Lord, to make an atonement with him, and to let him go for a scapegoat into the wilderness." Leviticus 16:7-10.

Once a year, on the great day of atonement, the high priest entered the most holy place for the cleansing of the sanctuary. The goat representing Jesus was slain and its blood was brought past the veil and sprinkled upon the mercy seat seven times. In this way an atonement was made for the most holy place. Then the high priest made an atonement for the holy place and the court, by placing the blood of the sin-offering seven times on each article of furniture.

"And Aaron shall lay both his hands upon the head of the live goat, and confess over him all the iniquities of the children of Israel, and all their transgressions in all their sins, putting them upon the head of the goat, and shall send him away by the hand of a fit man into the wilderness; and the goat shall bear upon him all their iniquities unto a land not inhabited." Verses 21, 22.

After sprinkling the blood seven times on the mercy seat in the most holy place, the high priest did a very special work. In his character of mediator he took all the sins that had symbolically accumulated in the most holy place upon himself and left the sanctuary. Symbolically he carried with him the burden of Israel's guilt and headed straight for the devil's goat—the scapegoat. In a very brief moment "all the iniquities of the children of Israel, and all their transgressions in all their sins" were put upon the head of the scapegoat, which represented the devil.

"Since Satan is the originator of sin, the direct instigator of all the sins that caused the death of the Son of God, justice demands that Satan shall suffer the final punishment. Christ's work for the redemption of men and the purification of the universe from sin, will be closed by the removal of sin from the heavenly sanctuary and the placing of these sins upon Satan, who will bear the final penalty." *Patriarchs and Prophets,* by Ellen G. White, page 358.

It is interesting to note that the word for goat in Hebrew is *sair.* In Leviticus 17:7 it says, "They shall no more offer their sacrifices to devils." The same Hebrew word is used here for devils—*sair.* We should always keep in mind that the devil's goat—the scapegoat—was not slain. The blood of that goat was not used. Only the Lord's goat was slain and its blood used to make atonement.

It seems almost blasphemous that Christ is going to take the full consequence of sin of which Satan has had a part in every person's life. When Christ paid the penalty on Calvary, He assumed the iniquities that Satan instigated. "Christ was made sin for us." Atonement at the mercy seat is really going to involve Christ assuming the sins of the entire world, which Satan had a part in instigating. One can only consider this as fantastic. It gives us an insight as to what God is doing for us to hazard His person to get us out of the situation of sin.

But how is the atonement of the earthly sanctuary fulfilled in Christ's ministry? We must never forget that the sanctuary in which Jesus ministers today in our behalf is the great original. The sanctuary built by Moses was only a copy. "Now when these things were thus ordained, the priests went always into the first tabernacle, accomplishing the service of God. But into the second went the high priest alone once every year, not without blood, which he offered for himself, and for the errors of the people: The Holy Ghost this signifying, that the way into the holiest of all was not yet made manifest, while as the first tabernacle was yet standing: Which was a figure for the time then present, in which were offered both gifts and sacrifices, that could not make him that did the service perfect, as pertaining to the conscience." Hebrews 9:6-9.

Here is introduced an element of the atonement that has not been characterized either by the blood on the altar in the courtyard or in the holy place. This involves the conscience of the individual—cleansing the conscience of guilt. The last work that God does for the human soul is to make the application of Christ's blood on the mercy seat in the most holy place making the conscience completely clear of any guilt of any involvement in sin. This is the final atonement. Isn't that wonderful?

Listen to this: "Ever since Adam's sin, the human race had been cut off from direct communion with God; the intercourse between heaven and earth had been through Christ; but now that Jesus had come 'in the likeness of sinful flesh,' the Father Himself spoke. He had before communicated with humanity *through* Christ; now He communicated with humanity *in* Christ." *The Desire of Ages,* page 116.

Today your High Priest, Jesus Christ, has now moved into the most holy place of the heavenly temple, where "thousand thousands minister unto him, and ten thousand times ten thousand stand before him." That temple filled with the glory of the eternal throne is where God is now dealing with the human race in the person of Christ's humanity. God's Son Jesus, in His humanity, suffered the guilt of the human race and He went down to eternal destruction, yet never once sinning. His blood shed on Calvary's cross claimed by you and applied by your High Priest in the heavenly sanctuary will cleanse the conscience, freeing it from any guilt and any involvement with sin.

Surely our heartcry today is: "Do it now, dear Saviour, and don't pass me by."

Pass Me Not

Pass me not, O Gentle Saviour,
Hear my humble cry.
While on others Thou art calling,
Do not pass me by.

Saviour, Saviour, hear my humble cry.
While on others Thou art calling,
Do not pass me by.

Trusting only in Thy merit
Would I seek Thy face;
Heal my wounded, broken spirit,
Save me by Thy grace.

Thou, the spring of all my comfort,
More than life to me.
Whom have I on earth beside Thee,
Whom in heaven but Thee?

Saviour, Saviour, hear my humble cry.
While on others Thou art calling,
Do not pass me by.

Chapter 10
Pattern of the Heavenly Sanctuary

Again we draw your attention to the sanctuary. But there are other sanctuaries than the one built by Moses that we would draw to your attention today. "Jesus answered and said unto them, Destroy this temple, and in three days I will raise it up. . . . But he spake of the temple of his body." John 2:19, 21. When Jesus stated that He will raise it up He had in mind His own person. He never intended to destroy the physical temple and certainly not to raise it up in three days. To make this point clear we are told, "And He spake of the temple of his body."

In a previous study we have shown that all the material for the structure that Moses built came from the people. The gold, silver, cloth, skins and jewels were given willingly when God said, "Let them make me a sanctuary." Exodus 25:8. It did not only pertain to the materialistic structure but to the aspect of the lineage of the coming of the Messiah. So as the people supplied the material for the building they also supplied the line of flesh and ancestry for the coming of the Messiah. It is the flesh symbol that Christ is referring to here in John

2:19. The Temple of His body symbolically met the fulfillment as a temple for God to dwell in.

Let us notice a statement that Christ made regarding His relationship to the temple. "But I say unto you, That in this place is one greater than the temple." Matthew 12:6. Christ had an occasion to make a comparison of Himself with the physical temple. There was a temple built by David which was destroyed by the Babylonians. This was rebuilt by Zerubbabel and was the one of which Christ spoke.

The sanctuary that Moses built was very intricate. "According to all that I shew thee, after the pattern of the tabernacle, and the pattern of all the instruments thereof, even so shall ye make it." Exodus 25:9. Moses followed a particular plan that God revealed to him, possibly a heavenly pattern. We understand that the sanctuary that Moses built and later on that David built had considerable differences but the basic principle of the apartments and its service was the same. Solomon had an observation that is applicable in relationship to the sanctuary. He said, "But will God indeed dwell on the earth? behold, the heaven and heaven of heavens cannot contain thee; how much less this house that I have builded?" 1 Kings 8:27. The great king recognized that God certainly wouldn't dwell fully in a building built by men on earth. There must be a greater sanctuary that God would occupy.

"But Christ being come an high priest of good things to come, by a greater and more perfect tabernacle, not made with hands, that is to say, not of this building." Hebrews 9:11. The sanctuary in which Jesus ministers today as our High Priest is the great original. The sanctuary built by Moses and later by David and Solomon were only copies.

"A minister of the sanctuary, and of the true tabernacle, which the Lord pitched, and not man." Hebrews 8:2. In this text a distinct difference is made between the heavenly temple and the mosaic temple. The people had brought the material and Bezaleel had been the superintendent. So it was definitely done by the hands of men.

But here is a sanctuary not built with the hands of men. This means more than just hands. It means beyond the power of human individuals. It is a heavenly structure. "The Lord pitched it."

Thoughtfulness would lead us to ask, "Are there sacrifices in the heavenly sanctuary too?" If we would say that lambs or animals are offered it would be contrary to the concepts that we have of heaven and its working principles. "It was therefore necessary that the patterns of things in the heavens should be purified with these; but the heavenly things themselves with better sacrifices than these." Hebrews 9:23.

Moses had been instructed to purify and cleanse the earthly sanctuary with the blood of bulls and goats. But the heavenly sanctuary was to be purified with better sacrifices than lambs, goats and bullocks, namely, the blood of Christ. His sacrifice was made on earth and was vastly superior to that of the animal sacrifices. But Christ's blood was applied in the heavenly sanctuary to do its work of purifying and cleansing. The blood of animals in the earthly sanctuary provided only ceremonial purity, whereas the blood of the new covenant, Christ's blood, provided moral purity and cleansing.

"For Christ is not entered into the holy places made with hands, which are the figures of the true; but into heaven itself, now to appear in the presence of God for us. Nor yet that he should offer himself often, as the high priest entereth into the holy place every year with blood of others; For then must he often have suffered since the foundation of the world: but now once in the end of the world hath he appeared to put away sin by the sacrifice of himself." Verses 24-26.

We need to emphasize the thought: Christ is now appearing in the "presence of God *for us.*" "He ever liveth to make intercession" for us. Hebrews 7:25. The reason we need someone to appear in the presence of God for us is that we have sinned. Christ "appeared to put away sin by the sacrifice of himself." Now this same Jesus, our High Priest, is ministering the benefits of His atonement in our behalf. As a result of this our mind, our conscience is "purged." Verse 14. The Greek word for "purged" is *katharizo.* It is used in verse 23 and translated "purified." It is also used again in 1 John 1:9 and translated "cleanse." So our precious Saviour and High Priest is ministering in the true tabernacle, appearing in the presence of God for us, interceding for us, and carrying on a work of cleansing that has to do with the sins of repentant men and women, boys and girls.

Just as the high priest in the earthly sanctuary on the Day of Atonement performed a special cleansing of the sanctuary, so Christ, "once in the end of the world," performs a special work of cleansing the heavenly sanctuary. This is predicted by Daniel the prophet. "Unto two thousand and three hundred days; then shall the sanctuary be cleansed." Daniel 8:14. When the Old Testament was written in Greek (the Septuagint version), the word used for "cleansed" was *katharizo.* (For additional information on the prophecy of the "2300 days," write for the book *End of the World Final Events,* by LaVerne E. Tucker.)

When the year-day principle is applied to the time period of 2300 days, the cleansing of the sanctuary was to begin in 1844 A.D. Of course, by that time the temple in Jerusalem had disappeared. Except for the yearly Day of Atonement service in the earthly sanctuary, all its services and sacrifices had pointed forward to the sacrifice of Christ on Calvary. When Christ died on the cross, the curtain or veil between the holy and most holy place in the temple in Jerusalem was torn "from the top to the bottom," signifying that the earthly sanctuary had come to its end. The Lamb of God had been slain. Therefore, the only sanctuary in existence in 1844 was the heavenly sanctuary, "the true tabernacle, which the Lord pitched, and not man." In a future study we will consider the meaning in more detail of why the heavenly sanctuary needed cleansing.

Christ as a sacrifice, Christ as a priest for our salvation! We must never lose sight of the fact that the humanity He inherited from His parents made this whole affair effective for us. "For the wages of sin is death; but the gift of God is eternal life through Jesus Christ our Lord." Romans 6:23. There is no animal that could meet this prerequisite. Only the man Jesus Christ could provide such a salvation.

The Old Testament had the same viewpoint on this matter. "And it was revealed in mine ears by the Lord of hosts, Surely this iniquity shall not be purged from you till ye die, saith the Lord God of hosts." Isaiah 22:14. The question can be asked, "Is it possible for the sinner to pay the penalty of his sin?" The answer is obviously, "Yes." But once he pays this penalty he is eternally lost. So a person could take his own blood and pay the penalty, but there would be no salvation.

This is the whole program of the sanctuary. God has come into our nature, picked up our humanity, taken our sins upon Himself and died the second death. This is the death that we should die if we do not accept His vicarious death. "But God commendeth his love toward us, in that, while we were yet sinners, Christ died for us." Romans 5:8. Here again we see the main plan of salvation. In order for Christ to die for us, He would have to take our nature upon Himself. This goes beyond animals, beyond the sanctuary on earth, and takes us into the sanctuary in heaven.

There are many people who do not believe that Christ died for them. And there may be some who do not care. When God deals with the world and sin and the great sacrifice that He made in Christ dying on Calvary, He is not going to permit the people who do not want to know or refuse to believe to evade this issue. They will at some time meet this issue. A case that illustrates this point is the sad story of Judas. For three whole years and more Judas had been with Jesus daily. Now we see him in anguish and hear his final words. "I have sinned in that I have betrayed the innocent blood. And they said, What is that to us? see thou to that." Matthew 27:4. As Judas witnessed how Jesus submitted to all the abuse that was heaped upon Him hour after hour, he could endure the torture of his guilty conscience no longer. And he cried out, "I have betrayed the innocent blood." Certainly Judas made a truthful statement. The blood of Christ's physical person was the only blood without the stain of guilt. Too late Judas came to recognize it.

People may say "I don't care. I am not concerned anyhow." But like Judas, there will come a time when every man, woman and child outside of Christ will realize that they should have cared, they should have been concerned. They should have accepted the blood that was shed for them.

Friend, let us make the right decision. Judas made the wrong one. He betrayed the innocent blood of Jesus. Let us today allow the blood of Jesus to wash away our sins. There is only one Man that has ever lived that sinless life and then died that we might live that life. Today as our High Priest, He lives for you and me, interceding for you, providing the power for you and me to live for Him. His name is Jesus. Accept Him today as your Saviour.

Jesus

The busy streets and sidewalks, they suddenly grew
    still
As a Man came thro' the entrance of the city,
As He touched and healed a blind man with a little piece
    of clay,
With trembling lips you could hear the people say:

Jesus, Jesus, He is the Son of God!
Jesus, Jesus, the precious Son of God!
Sweetest Rose of Sharon came to set us free;
Jesus, Jesus, He's everything to me,
Yes, He's all the world to me!

There are footprints in the sand along the Sea of Galilee
Where thousands came to hear and came to see Him;
There He taught of love and kindness, yes, He brought a
    better way,
As He spoke they'd turn and whisper and they'd say:

Jesus, Jesus, He is the Son of God!
Jesus, Jesus, the precious Son of God!
Sweetest Rose of Sharon came to set us free;
Jesus, Jesus, He's everything to me,
Yes, He's all the world to me!

Then the air grew cold and the sky turned black as
    they nailed Him to a tree,
There He died for ev'ry man and ev'ry country;
But the price He paid and the blood He shed is changing
    lives today,
And with joy and praise you can hear these people say:

Jesus, Jesus, He is the Son of God!
Jesus, Jesus, the precious Son of God!
Sweetest Rose of Sharon came to set us free;
Jesus, Jesus, He's everything to me,
Yes, He's all the world to me!

Chapter 11
Priests Are Chosen From Among Men

"Thy way, O God, is in the sanctuary." Through these studies we have found that the sanctuary truly reveals the eternal destiny open to every soul. In our study today we want to take a special look at the priests. Why did God choose the priest from among men?

"For every high priest taken from among men is ordained for men in things pertaining to God, that he may offer both gifts and sacrifices for sins." Hebrews 5:1. Immediately a person might ask "Where else would God get priests?" He could have taken them from angels or perhaps from another source. But the scripture says distinctly God is choosing them from among men and ordained them to serve men.

God gives some detailed instructions concerning the priests in the 18th chapter of Deuteronomy. "The priests the Levites, and all the tribe of Levi, shall have no part nor inheritance with Israel: they shall eat the offerings of the Lord made by fire, and his inheritance. Therefore shall they have no inheritance among their brethren: the Lord is their inheritance, as he hath said unto them. For the Lord thy God hath chosen him out of all thy tribes, to stand to minister in the name of the Lord, him and his sons for ever." Deuteronomy 18:1, 2, 5.

God chose the Levites as His priests. In the Hebrew language the word "priest" is *kohen* and means that the person is working for the benefit of others. The word "Levi" in Hebrew meant joined or to bring the person nigh. In this case the priest brings the person nigh to God. So the priest and Levi together means the priest works for the benefit of others to bring the people to God. Truly this is a privileged position to minister "in the name of the Lord" and represent His name. When you represent a person's name you are really representing their character. So the priests of the tribe of Levi were to reveal God's character and the whole subject of the sanctuary to bring the people to God. What a beautiful work to do.

"And I, behold, I have taken your brethren the Levites from among the children of Israel: to you they are given as a gift for the Lord, to do the service of the tabernacle of the congregation. Therefore thou and thy sons with thee shall keep your priest's office for every thing of the altar, and within the veil; and ye shall serve: I have given your priets's office unto you as a service of gift: and the stranger that cometh nigh shall be put to death." Numbers 18:6, 7.

You notice that the Levites are given to the people as a special gift. Always keep in mind that when we are talking about these priests, we are reflecting upon the position of Christ. These priests are representing what Christ has done, is doing, or is going to do. When it says the priest's work is to bring the people to God, that is exactly Christ's work—to bring the people to God.

In order to do this Christ would have to descend and take upon Himself the nature of human beings. This is why it says it will be a gift. It is the great gift of heaven to us. The Aaronic priesthood symbolizes Christ's ministry in our behalf to bring us from a condition of sin to God and eternal salvation. This priesthood is a blessed thing.

"All the best of the oil, and all the best of the wine, and of the wheat. And the firstfruits of them which they shall offer unto the Lord, them have I given thee." Verse 12.

The firstfruits of the grapes are very delicious. The grapes that ripen first and are put in the vat become choice grape juice. The priests were to have this because they were God's special gift. Recognizing this He gave them special gifts—the best of the oil, best of the wine, and best of the wheat. This is going to carry right on through this priesthood into the final consummation. The sanctuary reveals the destiny open to every human soul and this is one of the very distinct avenues of which this will be accomplished. It is plain to see that the priests were very privileged, but not only the priests.

"And ye shall be unto me a kingdom of priests, and an holy nation. These are the words which thou shalt speak unto the children of Israel." Exodus 19:6. God says the children of Israel were to be an holy nation and a special people. It is obvious that God had something in mind for them that was going to extend beyond this particular realm.

Underline in your Bible Isaiah 61:6. "But ye shall be named the Priests of the Lord: men shall call you the Ministers of our God: ye shall eat the riches of the Gentiles, and in their glory shall ye boast yourselves." Again God states that He has chosen these people to be ministers for Him. Shortly we will see that this particular service is not limited to the sanctuary, for when the priests bring God's people into the holiest place we are speaking of bringing them into the great confines of heaven and the magnificent service that they will serve there.

91

"But ye are a chosen generation, a royal priesthood, an holy nation, a peculiar people; that ye should shew forth the praises of him who hath called you out of darkness into his marvellous light." 1 Peter 2:9.

This is important: God has assigned the priests to lead Israel to the throne of God and to eternal salvation. God's redeemed become a royal priesthood. Royalty is kingship. "Jesus Christ . . . loved us, and washed us from our sins in his own blood, And hath made us kings and priests unto God and his Father." Revelation 1:5, 6. The redeemed of this earth shall become priests and kings.

Now it is time for us to take another look at the colors in the sanctuary doors—the entrances to each compartment. The priest always officiated in mercy (the blood) and in righteousness—the red and the blue. These when united make purple—the color of kings. So the priests are going right through these doors, bringing the people with them. They are going to perform a magnificent service not only in this world but priest and people will become "kings and priests" throughout the eternal ages.

In 1 Samuel 2:34 we are told that Hophni and Phinehas, the two wicked sons of Eli, the priest, will die because of their transgressions. The next verse states: "And I will raise me up a faithful priest, that shall do according to that which is in mine heart and in my mind: and I will build him a sure house; and he shall walk before mine anointed for ever." Verse 35. God will raise up a faithful priest that will do according to that which is in His heart—that which is in His mind. This means that the qualifications to be a priest was very high. In fact, the words "Holiness to the Lord," were to be written across their foreheads—their minds.

"And thou shalt make a plate of pure gold, and grave upon it, like the engravings of a signet, HOLINESS TO

THE LORD. And it shall be upon Aaron's forehead, that Aaron may bear the iniquity of the holy things, which the children of Israel shall hallow in all their gifts; and it shall be always upon his forehead, that they may be accepted before the Lord.'' Exodus 28:36, 38.

In one of our previous studies the point was made that Christ gave His mind a sacrifice for sin. It was in His mind that He bore the sins of the human race. Here is where that idea begins. The scripture says, ''Make a plate of pure gold . . . like the engravings of a signet, HOLINESS TO THE LORD. And it shall be upon Aaron's forehead.'' Because he has this ''HOLINESS TO THE LORD'' which God gives to him, it says that ''Aaron may bear the iniquity of the holy things.'' If he were not holy, and bearing iniquity, it would be disastrous. That's what happened to Nadab and Abihu. It is because of the quality of righteousness in his life that makes him able to bear the iniquity.

The qualifications and characteristics for the priesthood of believers is just as high as for the Aaronic priesthood. Every true believer in Christ—everyone who knows what it is to be washed in the blood of the Lamb and has yielded his life in full surrender to the will of God—makes up the priesthood of believers. They are the chosen generation, the royal priesthood, the holy nation. They are described in Revelation 20:6. ''Blessed and holy is he that hath part in the first resurrection: on such the second death hath no power, but they shall be priests of God and of Christ, and shall reign with him a thousand years.'' God employs them in a special service in His operation. The priests were taken from among men. So this priesthood of redeemed believers will be chosen from mankind and will do a special service of determining certain aspects of men's destiny during that thousand year period.

''And I saw a new heaven and a new earth: for the first

heaven and the first earth were passed away; and there was no more sea. And I John saw the holy city, new Jerusalem, coming down from God out of heaven prepared as a bride adorned for her husband. And I heard a great voice out of heaven saying, Behold, the tabernacle of God is with men, and he will dwell with them and they shall be his people, and God himself shall be with them, and be their God." Revelation 21:1-3.

The thousand year sojourn in heaven is over and God makes a new earth for His people where sin shall never arise again. But wonder of wonders, the entire Godhead—the Father, the Holy Spirit, and the Lamb—will make their headquarters on this little planet when it is all made new. "The tabernacle of God is with men." This tabernacle then constitutes His people—the royal priesthood, the peculiar people—and God is in their life. God has taken up His position of dwelling in this temple which constitutes His people. You can see how far this goes beyond the building—the sanctuary— in the wilderness of which we have been discussing. That was marvelous, but it doesn't compare with the excellency of the new earth, where God will dwell with and in that royal priesthood, that chosen people. They shall be "kings and priests" throughout all eternity.

"And I saw no temple therein: for the Lord God Almighty and the Lamb are the temple of it. And the city had no need of the sun, neither of the moon, to shine in it: for the glory of God did lighten it, and the Lamb is the light thereof. And the nations of them which are saved shall walk in the light of it: and the kings of the earth do bring their glory and honour into it." Verses 22-24.

We have been discussing the sanctuary. The Greek word *naos*, translated temple is the same word used for sanctuary when speaking of the holy and most holy places. The earthly sanctuary was symbolic of the dwelling place of God. But when sin shall be no more, God's people, the church, the royal priesthood will be able to dwell in His presence and no structure will be required to symbolize the dwelling of God, for "God Almighty and the Lamb are the temple."

What a marvelous destiny He has planned for you and me—"kings and priests" of God for all eternity. And we shall go right on serving Him forever, not because of fear but because of love. My friend, I'm sure you are planning to be there. We have made our decision. How about you? We are marching to Zion. Will you join us?

Come, we that love the Lord
And let our joys be known.
Join in a song with sweet accord,
Join in a song with sweet accord,
And thus surround the throne,
And thus surround the throne.

We're marching to Zion,
Beautiful, beautiful Zion,
We're marching upward to Zion,
The beautiful city of God.

Let those refuse to sing
Who never knew our God.
But children of the heavenly King,
But children of the heavenly King
May speak their joys abroad,
May speak their joys abroad.

Then let our songs abound
And every tear be dry.
We're marching through Emmanuel's ground,
We're marching through Emmanuel's ground,
To fairer worlds on high,
To fairer worlds on high.

Chapter 12
The Breastplate and Precious Stones

Twelve polished stones! They are chemically structured so that they are different. The polishing is what really makes them jewels. These 12 stones were carefully arranged in four rows on the multi-colored breastplate worn by Aaron, the high priest, in the sanctuary in the wilderness. What do these precious stones represent? Who do they represent? What about the Urim and Thummin—the large stones on the breastplate? What does the breastplate represent?

Our search for answers takes us first to Psalm 135:4. "For the Lord hath chosen Jacob unto himself, and Israel for his peculiar treasure." God has chosen Jacob. The moment David mentions Jacob he is touching on this breastplate, for Jacob is the father of the tribes of Israel. When he says that they are His "peculiar treasure," David is using terminology drawn from these precious stones of the breastplate. Israel in scripture represents all of God's people. When David said that God had chosen Jacob unto himself, it meant He had chosen the whole twelve tribes and they are a peculiar jewel or treasure to Him.

As you look at the twelve stones on the breastplate of the high priest you will notice that each one is different. Remember that it is the polishing that really makes them jewels. It is the hardships, the trials of life that build character. And it is through these trials, faithfully endured, that we are polished and finally brought into this breastplate.

It is important to keep in mind that when we speak of the Mosiac sanctuary we are also speaking about Christ and the heavenly sanctuary. When God speaks of twelve stones He is talking about the twelve tribes of Israel, and these twelve tribes represent every person upon the earth. So each one of us would be one of these twelve stones on the breastplate of the high priest.

"And the Lord your God will save them in that day as a flock of His people, for they are as the stones of a crown, sparkling in His land." Zechariah 9:16, NASE. God is going to save His people and they shall be like sparkling stones. Isn't it marvelous that God thinks of His redeemed as jewels? "And thou shalt set in it settings of stones, even four rows of stones: the first row shall be a sardius, a topaz, and a carbuncle: this shall be the first row. And the second row shall be an emerald, a sapphire, and a diamond. And the third row a ligure, an agate, and an amethyst. And the fourth row a beryl, and an onyx, and a jasper: they shall be set in gold in their enclosings. And the stones shall be with the names of the children of Israel, twelve, according to their names, like the engravings of a signet; every one with his name shall they be according to the twelve tribes." Exodus 28:17-21.

In comparing these precious stones with the precious stones in the twelve foundations of the wall of the New Jerusalem, you will find them similar in stones and colors, but arranged in different order (see Revelation 21:19, 20). On each stone on the high priest's breastplate was engraved a name of one of the tribes of Israel. These names engraved on the twelve jewels indicates the value of each person in the sight of our heavenly Father. God regards His people as precious gems. The fact that each of the twelve tribes was represented by a gem of its own, different from the others, lets us know that every individual Christian has his own distinct personality, his own beauty in Heaven's sight. A name has to do with character. It is character that counts with God.

Meaning of the Breastplate

The twelve precious stones were set in the breast-plate. The all blue outer garment worn by the high priest was known as the ephod. And the chief purpose of the ephod was to hold the breastplate, which was attached to it after it was put on. "And thou shalt make the breastplate of judgment with cunning work; after the work of the ephod thou shalt make it; of gold, of blue, and of purple, and of scarlet, and of fine twined linen, shalt thou make it." Exodus 28:15.

The breastplate was the most striking and brilliant part of the priest's attire. It was called "the breastplate of judgment." We understand judgment to mean to make some judicious decision on certain matters. With the precious stones representing the redeemed of Israel, God is going to use them in a matter of judgment.

"For he put on righteousness as a breastplate, and an helmet of salvation upon his head; and he put on the garments of vengeance for clothing, and was clad with zeal as a cloke." Isaiah 59:17. Here are character qualities represented by units of armor used in combat. A breastplate is used to deflect any missiles shot at a person.

Sin began in God's perfect universe. First Lucifer in heaven and then Adam and Eve on this newly created planet, Earth. God is going to protect Himself against that ever occuring again. You see where this breastplate could be used. You may ask, "Why would God need any kind of protection?" Or "How did Lucifer ever come to oppose God, when God created him perfect?" Or "How did Adam and Eve take a position of opposition to God when they were created in God's image?"

When God created them with the quality of freewill, with freedom of choice which is an aspect of love, God knew that this would be a risk; someone might choose wrong. Once sin occurred in His universe a plan was already formulated to meet it. A part of that plan included this breastplate. It would serve as a protection and shield from the onslaughts of the enemy. The plan was so great that it included final triumph, assuring the entire universe that sin would never rise up again. God will never force the issue. It is going to come as a result of God's love in dealing with His people.

Another reason for the breastplate being called "the breastplate of judgment" was because it served primarily for bearing the "Urim and the Thummim." "And thou shalt put in the breastplate of judgment the Urim and the Thummim; and they shall be upon Aaron's heart, when he goeth in before the Lord: and Aaron shall bear the judgment of the children of Israel upon his heart before the Lord continually." Exodus 28:30.

It is imperative that we keep in mind that the high priest represents Jesus Christ. The Urim and Thummim were upon Aaron's heart. This means upon the heart of Christ, our High Priest. The name "Urim" comes from the Hebrew *Ur,* which means light. To make this plural *im* is added, meaning lights. Since it is a blue stone, as we have found in our previous study, it would denote righteousness. And light means righteousness, too.

The Thummim comes from the Hebrew *tummim,*

which means perfection, but in a very distinct manner. You recall when God was speaking to Satan concerning Job, He said, "Have you seen my friend, Job, that perfect man?" That word "perfect" is this Thummim stone. There is a quality in Job that relates him to this stone. With all the trouble and ill treatment he incurred, Job said, "God, though You slay me, I will still trust You." How could you beat that for dedication?

It is important to realize that when Job is saying, "Though He slay me, yet will I trust Him," he is portraying Christ's experience from Gethsemane to Calvary. Now if Christ did not maintain that trust, we are all lost. So putting the two stones together and thinking of the character qualities they represent, he is one who has the light; but he has more than the light. He has the facts. But he has more than the facts; he has the revelation of truth. But he has more than the revelation of truth; he has a dedication—even if it took him to death, he would never turn from God. That is the quality of these stones.

"And he shall stand before Eleazar the priest, who shall ask counsel for him after the judgment of Urim before the Lord; at his word shall they go out, and at his word they shall come in, both he, and all the children of Israel with him, even all the congregation." Numbers 27:21. When the time came for new leadership to take the place of Moses in leading the children of Israel into the Promised Land, God instructed Moses to choose Joshua to be that leader. At a special ceremony of blessing, Moses transferred his leadership to Joshua. Whereas Moses had received much of his counsel directly from God, Joshua was to go to the high priest, Eleazar, as a mediator between him and God. The high priest, in turn, was to consult the Urim and Thummim. God would continue to give the counsel, but through the Urim and Thummim. It could very well be that the redeemed of this earth, serving as kings and priests, will be given Urim and Thummim to assist them in their judiciary operation and function for God's service to determine when beings throughout the universe shall go in and out. Why do you suppose God would take the people from this earth and give them that particular position?

They have had an experience no other being in His universe, save Jesus, has had. Take the experience of Job. How could angels have the experience of Job? They don't know what it is to have sores and boils all over them. They don't know what it is to be redeemed. Nobody can understand like one who understands from the inside out. That is why the people who are redeemed from this earth, who have been through an experience on this earth which created beings in other realms of God's universe have never experienced will be given the responsibility doing a work of judgment in the kingdom to come (see 1 Corinthians 6:2).

"And of Levi he said, Let thy Thummim and thy Urim be with thy holy one, whom thou didst prove at Massah, and with whom thou didst strive at the waters of Meribah: Who said unto his father and to his mother, I have not seen him; neither did he acknowledge his brethren, nor knew his own children: for they have observed thy word, and kept thy covenant. They shall teach Jacob thy judgments, and Israel thy law: they shall put incense before thee, and whole burnt sacrifice upon thine altar." Deuteronomy 33:8-10. The scripture says they will teach the people. Those who have the Light and His righteousness, those who have His judgment, God is going to use in a very special way.

One day the disciple Simon Peter asked a question of Jesus and the Master gave a most interesting answer. "Peter . . . said unto him, Behold, we have forsaken all, and followed thee; what shall we have therefore? And Jesus said unto them, Verily I say unto you, that ye which have followed me, in the regeneration when the Son of man shall sit in the throne of his glory, ye also shall sit upon twelve thrones, judging the twelve tribes of Israel." Matthew 19:27, 28. Only through the experience on this earth of developing traits of character that show a complete dependence upon God for righteousness and judgment, symbolized in the breastplate of the high priest, is what prepares those who will do this work of judging in God's kingdom to come.

"And there shall be no more curse: but the throne of God and of the Lamb shall be in it; and his servants shall serve him: And they shall see his face; and his name shall be in their foreheads." Revelation 22:3, 4. The redeemed of this earth will serve our eternal Father and Saviour as kings and priests in a place where sin will never rise up again, because we have been fully restored to the image of God. Friend, this is God's plan for you! Have you made the choice to be there? Or are you still serving the world? What choice will you make. Will you take Jesus or will you continue to serve self and the world? We have made our choice and it is a good way to live. We invite you to make your choice with Jesus.

I'd Rather Have Jesus

I'd rather have Jesus than silver or gold,
I'd rather be His than have riches untold,
I'd rather have Jesus than houses or lands,
I'd rather be led by His nail-pierced hands.

Than to be the king of a vast domain,
Or be held in sin's dread sway.
I'd rather have Jesus than anything
This world affords today.

I'd rather have Jesus than men's applause,
I'd rather be faithful to His dear cause,
I'd rather have Jesus than worldwide fame,
I'd rather be true to His holy name.

Than to be the king of a vast domain,
Or be held in sin's dread sway.
I'd rather have Jesus than anything
This world affords today.

Chapter 13
The Sanctuary Summarized

The study of the sanctuary subject is like a vast ocean and we have only waded in knee deep in our past twelve visits together. However, what we have learned will be better remembered if we spend twenty minutes in summarizing what we have studied. There is a danger that we relegate the sanctuary to Old Testament times not realizing that God had the sanctuary built for all mankind. He planned its detailed services to reveal His relationship with man and how man can have a more intimate relationship with God and thereby live again with Him.

First, what was the setting for the erection of that first earthly sanctuary? For more than two hundred years the descendants of Abraham, Isaac and Jacob lived in Egypt surrounded by heathen worship and lifestyle. When God called Moses to lead the children of Israel out of Egypt into the land of Canaan, many of those 600,000 men and their families had lost all knowledge of the living God and the plan of salvation. In the spring of 1445 B.C., the children of Israel walked out of Egypt, crossed the Red Sea and camped at the foot of Mount Sinai. Here God planned to reveal to the children of Israel that they were His chosen people and His entire plan of salvation. It was an elaborate system of teaching by illustration.

God said to Moses, "Let them make me a sanctuary; that I may dwell among them." Exodus 25:8. The material for the sanctuary structure and furniture came from the people—what they had brought with them. Many of their Egyptian neighbors and friends had given them going away gifts. All of these were gladly brought and given for the erection of the sanctuary. Each detail of the structure and furniture was given by God to Moses. It was built for God's presence. When it was finished, it was anointed and dedicated and the actual presence of God came into the building and took His position in the most holy place. His presence was indicated by the pillar of cloud over the ark of the covenant by day and a pillar of fire by night. This was the actual presence of Deity.

In the structure there were three curtains for doors. One curtain was at the entrance into the courtyard. The second separated the courtyard from the holy place, and the third separated the holy place from the most holy place. The latter two compartments were known as the tabernacle, and years later known as the temple.

In the Hebrew language these particular doors carried the meaning of thinking or decision. As the person stood outside he was to make a decision to come into the court. Christ said, "I am the door." The individual must make a decision to accept by faith the coming Messiah as his personal Saviour. As he did he stepped through the door separating him from the outside into the court area where Christ's righteousness was given to him as a gift. He is, in the sight of God, as righteous as Christ is righteous. Christ's righteousness was symbolized to the children of Israel by the white fence or wall that surrounded the courtyard.

Now the individual had another decision to make, represented by the second door. As he stood in the courtyard he must make the decision to demonstrate that righteousness by obedience. When that decision is made he steps through the door into the holy place. The holy place was surrounded by a gold wall which represented God's love to the human race.

At this point a person should make a very important interpretation. It is in the courtyard that Christ gives by faith His righteousness to the individual. In the holy place he maintains that righteousness by the administration of the high priest, in cooperation with the dynamic working of the Holy Spirit in his yielded life demonstrating obedience to the law of God. The high priest, who represents Christ, supplements the righteousness which the individual lacks, always keeping his character up to the stature of the gold wall of perfection.

When the individual believes in Christ's blood on Calvary as payment for his sins and steps through the door into the most holy place, Christ will put His blood shed on Calvary on the lid of the ark—the mercy seat—and that blood will wipe away all of man's guilt.

In addition to the three doors there are a number of pieces of furniture in the sanctuary. There are two articles of furniture in the court—the altar of burnt offering made of acacia wood and overlaid with bronze, and the laver made of bronze—which have reference to Christ's life. When Jesus died on Calvary "one of the soldiers with a spear pierced his side, and forthwith came there out blood and water." John 19:34. These two articles of furniture represented that blood and water—a specific work of Christ for the sinner's salvation.

Three articles of furniture were located in the holy place. On the north wall was the table of showbread or bread of His Presence. The table was made of acacia wood overlaid with gold. Twelve loaves or cakes of unleavened bread, replaced each Sabbath, were a perpetual thank offering to God for the twelve tribes for the blessings of life they received daily from Him. This bread represented Christ's body, for Jesus said, "Unless you eat my flesh, you have no part with me."

Across from the table of showbread, on the south wall, was the seven-branched candlestick made of a talent of pure gold (Exodus 25:31-40). These seven lamps were continually burning and represented Jesus. He said, "I am the light of the world," "the light of life." When we accept Christ as our Saviour we become a light reflecting His glory.

The third article of furniture was the altar of incense placed before the veil that divided the holy place from the most holy place. Though located in the holy place it was considered as belonging to the most holy place (Hebrews 9:3, 4). The altar of incense was made of acacia wood overlaid with pure gold. "The incense, ascending with the prayers of Israel, represents the merits and intercession of Christ, his perfect righteousness, which through faith is imputed to his people, and which can alone make the worship of sinful beings acceptable to God. Before the vail of the most holy place, was an altar of perpetual intercession, before the holy (place), was an altar of continual atonement. By blood and by incense, God was to be approached,—symbols pointing to the great Mediator, through whom sinners may approach Jehovah, and through whom alone mercy and salvation can be granted to the repentant, believing soul." E. G. White, *Patriarchs and Prophets,* page 353.

In the most holy place was the ark of the covenant, a chest made of acacia wood overlaid with pure gold. Inside the ark was placed the law of God—two tables of stone upon which was written with the finger of God the Ten Commandments. The lid of this chest, considered as another article of furniture, was made of pure gold and known as the mercy seat. Upon the mercy seat rested two sculptured cherubims of gold, both looking down upon the mercy seat and the law of God below.

When a person recognizes the law that Christ has written in his heart to be a transcript of God's character and the great standard of His rule, the Christian chooses to obey that law. However, at various times he falls short of full obedience and repents of his sins, Christ puts His blood shed on Calvary on the mercy seat and cleanses him of all guilt of sin. The sanctuary is revealing the great plan of salvation for the human soul. A person moves through the sanctuary by believing in Christ and accepting His righteousness by faith. Stepping into the holy place he allows Christ to live out His obedient life in him through the Holy Spirit. Finally he steps into the most holy place where the final atonement will be made as Christ puts the blood of Calvary on the mercy seat to cleanse the Christian of all human guilt. Walking through these three doors with Christ is experiencing the three phases of salvation—justification, sanctification, and finally glorification. And Jesus has provided it all!

ALMA: Pastor Lewis, I would like to have you go through this again and make plain the special work Christ does in the court, the holy place and the most holy place.

PASTOR LEWIS: In the courtyard, when the person steps through the door, Christ takes the person's sins and places them on the altar, which represents Calvary and in turn gives to the individual His righteousness. This is given to him by faith as an outright gift called righteousness by faith. As the individual steps through the door into the holy place, the righteousness that Christ gave him in the court will now maintain his life so he could be said to be obedient to the law of God, as God said of David. ". . . David, who kept my commandments, and who followed me with all of his heart, who only did that which was right in mine eyes." 1 Kings 14:8.

Now if a person dies and has not achieved absolute perfection of conduct, but his life has been lived in the holy place experience—the righteousness of Christ is maintaining his life—when his name comes up in the most holy place judgment, Christ stands or represents him and makes up anything he lacks in the sense of righteousness, blots away all the consequences of sin, and the person will be as if he had never sinned.

NEVA COYLE: Why are there two apartments within the area of the gold wall?

PASTOR LEWIS: Christ encouraged the church of Laodicea to buy of Him gold tried in the fire, white raiment and eyesalve (Revelation 3:18). The white raiment represented the righteousness of Christ, and the "gold tried in the fire" represented "faith which worketh by love" (Galatians 5:6) and the works that result from faith—obedience. As we have pointed out, the white fence or wall around the court represents the righteousness of Christ. The gold wall represents Christ living out His obedient life in the individual by faith. Jesus said, "If ye love me, keep my commandments." John 14:15. The gold wall of loving obedience was divided by a veil making two apartments. The reason for that is so you can recognize where the law of God is located. The person must come to absolute perfection to be in the most holy place. But inasmuch as he is endeavoring to live the Christian life and does not always come to absolute perfection, then his experience is that of the holy place.

The thought is expressed in the second chapter of Ephesians that when Christ died on Calvary He overcame the enmity and took away the middle wall of partition, making of twain one apartment. So the individual, if he dies in the holy place experience and there is sin in his life, is in a position of righteousness and sin. But when the Lord does His finishing work in the most holy place and wipes all the sin away, the veil is taken away and his life is completely gold. So while the person is endeavoring to live the Christian life but does not fully do it, he is typified by the partition between the holy and most holy place. It indicated that the holy place was not in accord with the most holy place where the law of God was located. But in the course of time, when Christ suffered the enmity of sinners and died for the sins of the whole world, the veil was rent in two and Christ made the two apartments into one. This demonstrates what He will do in every person's life.

PASTOR TUCKER: Where would you calculate the body of believers are in their movement through the sanctuary?

PASTOR LEWIS: If the person has had the experience we call conversion—accepting Christ as his personal Saviour—he is considered in the courtyard. If the person then endeavors to live the Christian life, to carry out what Christ has given to him in his conduct of daily living, that would put him in the holy place. That is where most people are in their Christian life. They would never move into the most holy place until the judgment and the coming of Christ or until they have reached absolute perfection of conduct, and that disqualifies most persons. So most of the Christian people today are in the holy place experience, letting their light shine to a certain extent, eating of the bread of heaven, the Word of God, and by prayer keeping in contact with God.

We can be thankful that there was one Person, Jesus Christ, who came and lived the perfect life and could therefore go on through into the most holy place. And because of Him and through His righteousness only, imputed and imparted, we can be victorious too!

ALMA: Why was it that in the time when the sanctuary was in the wilderness the people could only go into the outer court area but the priest went into the apartments?

PASTOR LEWIS: The holy place and the most holy place had a covering over them which represents heaven. The gold wall represents the loving obedience and righteous conditions of heaven. The brass or bronze furniture in the courtyard represents the condition of the people in somewhat of an imperfect state, as brass would be in comparison with gold. There was no ceiling on the courtyard so the people could see what was happening. This typified earth. Only in a vicarious way, through the priest, could the people go into the holy and most holy places which represented heaven.

PASTOR TUCKER: It might be well for us to think together for a few moments on the subject of What is Christ doing now in the heavenly sanctuary?

PASTOR LEWIS: Briefly stated, when Christ finished His work in the courtyard—His incarnation, living a sinless life, His death, burial and resurrection—He returned to the heavenly sanctuary. The apostle John, in vision on the Isle of Patmos, saw Jesus in the holy place of the heavenly sanctuary among the seven golden candlesticks (Revelation 1:10-13). Later in vision, when it was time for the dead to "be judged," John saw the "temple of God was opened in heaven, and there was seen in his temple the ark of his testament." Revelation 11:18, 19. This would be the most holy place. Today Christ is in the most holy place making the final arrangements for persons who have trust in Him. So the work in the heavenly sanctuary is in the last area at the present time. But that does not keep Him from accepting every person who comes to Him by faith and giving His righteousness to that person. He also continues to live

His obedient life in every child of God who chooses to live only to please the Master. One of these days very soon Christ will stand up and make an announcement that will bring to a close this special work in the most holy place: "He that is unjust, let him be unjust still: and he which is filthy, let him be filthy still: and he that is righteous, let him be righteous still: and he that is holy, let him be holy still. And, behold, I come quickly; and my reward is with me, to give every man according as his work shall be." Revelation 22:11, 12. Christ's work as Mediator, Intercessor and Advocate will be completed, and He will come as King of kings and Lord of lords to take home to heaven all who have put their complete trust in Him and have been judged worthy—having His complete robe of righteousness.

PASTOR TUCKER: It must be significant that the furniture in the court was made of bronze or brass, while in the other areas the furniture was gold.

PASTOR LEWIS: If a person had a finely polished brass object it would look much like gold. If you had alternating objects of gold and brass, it might be difficult to tell the difference. Although a person has received the righteousness of Christ it may not be genuinely assimilated into his life. But as he steps into the holy place that righteousness of Christ becomes more completely assimilated until the image of Jesus is fully reflected in his life—solid gold! Day by day the character of Christ is assimilated. The beauty of holiness is growing in the life. Christ continues to live His beautiful, obedient life in the one who completely yields his will to the Master. And the Master sustains, maintains and upholds him.

NEVA COYLE: Does a person go into the sanctuary in his experience and then go out again? Is there a revolving door?

PASTOR LEWIS: This is true in the Christian experience all too often. Some people begin a relationship with God and for some reason give it up and leave. These doors as I have explained are doors of life approaching God. If a person gets into the courtyard or into the holy place and chooses to go out, then the doors are a symbol of death. They are life going in and death going out. In many instances, if a person goes out that door is closed. In the story of the ten virgins, when they came back from buying oil the door was closed. It is a dangerous plan to turn your back on God.

PASTOR TUCKER: What we are talking about is a relationship of faith and trust.

PASTOR LEWIS: Yes, every door is faith. The word for door is belief—faith. First, a person accepts Christ as his personal Saviour by faith. Second, by faith he must move into obedience. Third, by faith he must know that Christ on Calvary paid the penalty of his guilt, and in the day of rewards he will experience eternal life with Christ on His throne. So the person who exhibits faith in Christ and who keeps confidence in God, assimilating His character each day, the Lord will see to it he will walk the streets of gold.

PASTOR TUCKER: Friend, do you have that faith? Dr. Graham Maxwell says that faith is the only prerequisite needed for heaven. So I ask you, Do you have that personal relationship with Christ? If not, I invite you to begin that relationship by yielding your life to Him and then keep on trusting Him.

Only Trust Him

Come, ev'ry soul by sin oppressed,
There's mercy with the Lord.
And He will surely give you rest
By trusting in His word.

Only trust Him, Only trust Him,
Only trust Him now.
He will save you, He will save you,
He will save you now.

Come, then and join this holy band,
And on to glory go,
To dwell in that celestial land
Where joys immortal flow.

Chapter 14
Cleansing of the Sanctuary

In Daniel 8:12 we find the prophecy that the truth of God's sanctuary in heaven was to be cast to the ground. In verse 13 the question is asked "How long will the truth be trampled into the dust?" Back came the answer, "Unto two thousand and three hundred days; then shall the sanctuary be cleansed." Daniel 8:14.

That word "cleansed" comes from a Hebrew word *nitsdaq* which literally translated would be "then shall the sanctuary be made righteous." But the sanctuary is a building, and neither in English nor in Hebrew are buildings ordinarily made righteous! So some translators have struggled with the alternate words, "justified" and "just"; and when these haven't seemed to help much, they have tried synonyms and come up with "vindicate" and even "emerge victorious." That is why one of the preferred translations has the passage "then the sanctuary shall be restored to its rightful state." One thing for sure, Gabriel knew that Daniel could understand the passage without specific interpretation, so now we want to know how other Jews who lived long ago understood it.

We are fascinated to discover that in both of the

translations that were made into Greek in ancient times by Jewish scholars, the word *nitsdaq* is translated by an ordinary word meaning "cleansed," the same meaning as in the King James Version. It is interesting to note that when the celebrated Christian scholar, Jerome, translated this passage into Latin around the year A.D. 400, after holding extensive conversations with a Jewish rabbi in regard to the Old Testament idioms, he chose the Latin word that also means "cleansed."

With this background and the careful study of the previous 13 chapters,we want to know what these words really mean, "then shall the sanctuary be cleansed" and when it will be cleansed?

The Meaning of "Sanctuary Cleansed"

Daily the priests offered the morning and evening sacrifices in the court of the sanctuary for the sins of the congregation. And daily the people brought their sacrifices for their sins and took the life of a lamb to show their faith in the coming death of the Son of God. These sins would accumulate in the sanctuary and on one day each year the children of Israel held the solemn and sacred services of the Day of Atonement or the Day of Judgment.

Jewish people who understand the background and reasons for their system of worship will tell you that their Day of Atonement was originally given to decide who would be worthy to pass into the promised land. Do you see, all whose sins did not get into the sanctuary during the year naturally would not have been forgiven, for they were not present when the cleansing took place on this Day of Cleansing or Day of Judgment.

From our previous study of the book of Hebrews (chapters 8 and 9) we have found that this system of sacrifices and the sanctuary services of the Old Testament times were but a MINIATURE—a kindergarten illustration—of the great work of our Lord Jesus Christ who is now pleading His blood in the sanctuary above for our sins. See Hebrews 8:1, 2; 9:11, 12, 25-27.

A Day Equals a Year in Prophecy

Just as the carpenters, in building a house, find written upon the blueprints the scale of ¼ inch equals 1 foot; so God has His scale, His yardstick, by which we are to measure the time periods in Bible prophecy. In Ezekiel 4:6 we are told that a day represents a year in prophecy. Therefore, 2300 days would equal 2300 years, using God's prophetic yardstick. But Daniel faints when he sees the events that will transpire during this long time period. He sees the horrible death, crucifixion of his long-looked-for Messiah. But Daniel recovers, does the king's business, but is much troubled about the vision of the 2300 days. So, Daniel prays.

Friend, that is a good thing to do. When you do not understand something; when everything seems to be going wrong; when business has failed; friends have failed you; when it seems like God has forsaken you— pray! So, Daniel prayed: O God, help me to understand this time period. And the scripture says in Daniel 9:22 that while Daniel was still praying, the answer came. God heard Daniel's prayer and said: Gabriel, there is a man down there that I love. He's asked for wisdom and understanding. Go down and tell Daniel what that vision means. And while Daniel is still praying, Gabriel comes down and says: "Daniel, I am now come forth to give thee skill and understanding."

490 Years Cut Off for Jewish Nation

The angel Gabriel immediately begins where he left off. "Seventy weeks are determined [cut off] upon thy people and upon thy holy city, to finish the transgression, and to make an end of sins, and to make

117

reconciliation for iniquity, and to bring in everlasting righteousness, and to seal up the vision and prophecy, and to anoint the most Holy." Daniel 9:24. The angel continues to explain the prophecy to Daniel. "Know therefore and understand, that from the going forth of the commandment to restore and to build Jerusalem unto the Messiah the Prince shall be seven weeks, and threescore and two weeks." Verse 25.

Now 70 weeks is a very definite and distinct period of time. These 70 weeks are cut off from the 2300 days or 2300 years. How many days are there in a week? Seven. And 7 times 70 is 490 days. Remember in the calculation of Bible prophecy, a day stands for a year. So 490 days would really be 490 years. The period of time listed in the 25th verse is just one week less—"seven weeks" plus "three score" (60) "and two weeks." This equals 69 weeks. How many years is this? Sixty-nine times seven gives us 483 days or 483 years from the "commandment to restore and build Jerusalem unto the Messiah the Prince."

But when does the time period begin? When was the final command given to restore and build Jerusalem? In Ezra 7:7, 13 we read: "In the seventh year of Artaxerxes the king [of Persia] . . . I make a decree, that all they of the people of Israel . . . go up to Jerusalem." Here is the decree to go and build Jerusalem. Now the actual date has been confirmed in many ways. The date given in my Bible margin is 457 B.C. The seventh year of the reign of Artaxerxes would also give us 457 B.C. because he began his rule in 464 B.C. Starting with the date 457 B.C., in the fall of the year when the decree went into effect, we travel down the corridors of time 483 years, which brings us to a glorious event in the annals of history.

In Luke 3:1 we have this important information: "Now in the fifteenth year of the reign of Tiberius

Caesar, Pontius Pilate being governor of Judea . . ." History tells us that Tiberius Caesar began his rule in 12 A.D. and by adding 15 years would give us the date 27 A.D. What happened in that year? Notice verse 21: "Now when all the people were baptized, it came to pass, that Jesus also being baptized, and praying, the heaven was opened, and the Holy Ghost descended in a bodily shape like a dove upon him, and a voice came from heaven, which said, Thou art my beloved Son; in thee I am well pleased." The 483 years have come to an end and Jesus, the Messiah, is anointed at His baptism.

Immediately following His baptism, Jesus was taken by the Spirit into the wilderness and following His short stay there, He came back and began preaching. Notice Mark 1:14, 15. Jesus came "preaching the gospel of the kingdom of God, and saying, The time is fulfilled!" What time? The 69 weeks—483 years—are fulfilled. Exactly on time, God's great time clock strikes the hour, 27 A.D., and Jesus appears, is baptized, is anointed by the Holy Ghost, and begins His ministry.

70 Weeks End in 34 A.D.

Remember the prophecy said: "Seventy weeks are determined [or cut-off]" for the Jewish nation. The difference between 69 weeks and 70 weeks is one week—7 prophetic days which equal 7 years. By adding 7 years to the date 27 A.D., we arrive at 34 A.D. What happened in A.D. 34? The special day of opportunity given to the Jewish nation came to an end and the apostles began to teach the gospel to the Gentiles. When Stephen was addressing his message of a crucified and risen Saviour clearly and definitely to the Jewish Sanhedrin, they rushed upon him and he was stoned, the first Christian martyr. That climaxed the 490 years allotted to the nation Israel.

In A.D. 34 the gospel began to go to the Gentiles. And

who was the one whom God called especially for that work? You will remember, when Stephen was stoned, "the witnesses laid down their clothes at a young man's feet, whose name was Saul" of Tarsus. (See Acts 7:58.) He was a prominent Pharisee, brilliant and fearless. But on his way to Damascus to kill more Christians, Saul came face to face with Jesus. It is a thrilling story of conversion: That bright light from heaven blinding Saul; the voice of Jesus saying, "Saul, Saul, why persecutest thou me? And he said, Who art thou, Lord? And the Lord said, I am Jesus whom thou persecutest. . . . And he trembling and astonished said, Lord what wilt thou have me to do?" Acts 9:4-6. From that day on, Saul, whose name was changed to Paul, preached Christ and Him crucified. He became the great apostle to the Gentiles. 34 A.D. marks the beginning of the gospel going to the Gentiles.

Truth To Be Restored in 1844

Now the 490 years are over. These 490 years were cut off from the 2300 years. Subtract 490 from 2300 and you have 1810 years left. Now add these 1810 years to 34 A.D. and this brings us to the year 1844. What was to happen then? Daniel 8:14 says: "Unto two thousand and three hundred days; then shall the sanctuary be cleansed." But also, the truth that had been trampled into the ground was to come to the light of the world. God's truth concerning the heavenly sanctuary was to be cast to the ground by a religious-political power (Daniel 8:11, 12). How long was this to go on? How long before God's truth was to be revealed? Until 1844. Then God's last warning message was go to the world—the truth concerning the heavenly sanctuary was be preached.

Christ Cut Off in Midst of Week

Purposely I have left out the very heart of this

prophecy until this point. Daniel 9:26, 27 tells what was to happen in the middle of this seventieth week. It says "shall Messiah be cut off, but not for himself: . . . And he shall confirm the covenant with many for one week [or 7 years of prophecy]: and in the midst of the week he shall cause the sacrifice and the oblation to cease."

For hundreds of years, the Jewish people had been bringing a little innocent lamb morning and night to the door of the earthly sanctuary for a sacrifice for their sins. But this text says the time will come when Christ, "in the midst of the week, shall cause the sacrifice [of lambs] to cease." What was the purpose of the sacrificed lamb? It pointed forward to the Lamb of God. When Jesus was baptized by John the Baptist, John said: "Behold the Lamb of God, which taketh away the sin of the world." John 1:29. But now, in the midst of the week, Jesus stops all this sacrificing of lambs. How?

Come with me to that upper room as Jesus washes the disciples' feet and institutes the Lord's supper. Let us follow the Saviour as He makes His way to the Garden of Gethsemane. There He prays, He agonizes. There He is betrayed. We follow to Pilate's Judgment Hall and witness the greatest legal farce of all time. Jesus is spit upon, cursed, beaten, scourged. A crown of thorns is jammed upon His head. He wears a purple robe. Then the mob cries out: "Hail, King of the Jews!" They smite Him again and again. Finally the cry goes out: "Crucify Him, crucify Him!" See Him trudge up Calvary; see Him nailed to the cross: those huge nails pierce those hands that have ministered to the needs of others—outstretched time and time again in healing the sick, in blessing the little children. Then the nails are driven through those feet that have traveled the dusty roads of Palestine on errands of mercy. The cross is lifted and dropped in the hole, tearing His flesh.

We read in Matthew 27:50 and 51: "Jesus, when he

had cried again with a loud voice, yielded up the ghost. And, behold, the veil of the temple was rent in twain from the top to the bottom." What did this signify? When Jesus cried: "It is finished!" and died, Christ's death brought to an end the entire service of the earthly sanctuary. There was no more a need to sacrifice lambs, which pointed forward to the time when Jesus would die for the sins of the world. Why? Because out there on yonder cross, the true Lamb of God, the Saviour of the world, died! The Lamb of God had paid the price! He died for your sins and mine.

Listen to His words as He gently prays: "Father, forgive them; for they know not what they do." Now He cries aloud: "My God, my God, why hast thou forsaken me?" As the darkness engulfs the cross, He speaks again, "It is finished!" And He bows His head and dies for you and for me!

For 3½ years, by Christ's own ministry, He had confirmed the covenant with the Jewish nation. Then, the disciples confirmed the covenant with the Jewish nation for 3½ years more. In the very midst of the seven-year period, just 3½ years from the beginning of His ministry, Jesus was cut off—31 A.D., in the spring of the year. The hour had struck! The Lamb was slain!

Can anyone doubt His divinity? Can anyone doubt this prophecy? Why, friend, this prophecy is sealed with the precious blood of Jesus! This prophecy is certain! This prophecy rivets my faith in Jesus. Jesus Christ is my Lord, my God! Every date, every event is sure! Jesus Christ was baptized and anointed in 27 A.D. H was crucified in the middle of that prophetic, 70th week—31 A.D. In 34 A.D. Stephen was stoned and the gospel began to be preached to the Gentile world. In 1844 A.D., at the end of the 2300 years, the judgment began in the heavenly sanctuary. What makes this prophecy certain? It is sealed with the precious blood of Jesus!

The hour had struck when the great Day of Atonement—the day of judgment—was to begin! This does not in the least date the second coming of Christ. A.D. 1844 marks the beginning of the investigative judgment in the heavens. This is the last and latest prophetic date in the Bible. We are living in the last days. Since 1844 time has been stretching out like a rubber band. Soon Jesus' mercy will have reached its limit when every soul will have had full and ample opportunity to surrender to Him. Then the end will come.

Investigative Judgment Described

John the Beloved looked forward to the time of judgment. He saw a great stirring taking place. Underline in your Bible Revelation 14:6, 7. The prophet saw a great message begin to go "to every nation, kindred, tongue, and people." What was the message? "Fear God, and give glory to him; for the hour of his judgment is come: and worship him that made heaven, and earth, and the sea, and the fountains of waters."

Notice the words carefully: "The hour of his judgment IS come." Not HAS come—something back in the past; nor WILL come—something away off in the future. But IS COME! The Lord did not allow 1844 to pass without proclaiming to the world that this great court was

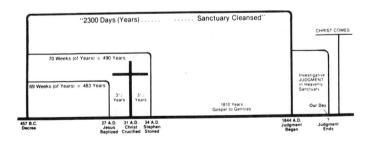

"2300 Days (Years) . . . . Sanctuary Cleansed"

CHRIST COMES

70 Weeks (of Years) = 490 Years

69 Weeks (of Years) = 483 Years

Investigative JUDGMENT in Heavenly Sanctuary

3½ Years   3½ Years

1810 Years
Gospel to Gentiles

Our Day

| 457 B.C. Decree | 27 A.D. Jesus Baptized | 31 A.D. Christ Crucified | 34 A.D. Stephen Stoned | 1844 A.D. Judgment Began | ? Judgment Ends |

123

beginning its session. "Surely the Lord God will do nothing, but he revealeth his secret unto his servants the prophets." Amos 3:7.

God did not allow that great event to go by without revealing it to His servants. In America 700 ministers of all different denominations and in Europe 300 ministers began to preach "The Hour of His Judgment Is Come!" It was the greatest revival since the time of the apostles, and that work has been continued down to the present time.

There are three phases to every trial in our earthly courts. There is the trial proper, or as it is sometimes called, the investigation. There is the decision, or verdict. And there is the executive phase—the execution of the decree of the judge. So it is in the heavenly court. The investigative part is NOW in progress. The Bible makes it very clear that when Jesus returns the verdict has already been made and He brings His rewards with Him. "He that is unjust, let him be unjust still: and he which is filthy, let him be filthy still: and he that is righteous, let him be righteous still: and he that is holy, let him be holy still. And, behold, I come quickly; and my reward is with me, to give every man according as his work shall be." Revelation 22:11, 12.

Of course, God does not need an investigation for Him to know who is to receive the reward of life everlasting. But there is an enemy that is accusing God of being unjust. This investigative judgment is for his benefit and for yours and mine. Therefore the investigative phase of the judgment has been in progress prior to His return, else how could the decree go forth: He that is unjust, or he that is righteous, let him remain that way?

Just as the great Day of Atonement was to decide who should continue into the promised land, so the great Day of Atonement in the heavens is a time of investigation to discover what the verdict shall be who will be worthy to go to the heavenly promised land. When Jesus returns the verdict is made very plain and then follows the execution of His plans. The righteous are led into life eternal and the wicked receive their punishment.

Judgment Set, Books Opened

Come with me, friend, and let us view this heavenly court scene. "I beheld till the thrones were cast down, and the Ancient of days did sit, whose garment was white as snow, and the hair of his head like the pure wool: his throne was like the fiery flame, and his wheels as burning fire. A fiery stream issued and came forth from before him: thousand thousands ministered unto him, and ten thousand times ten thousand stood before him: the judgment was set, and the books were opened." Daniel 7:9, 10.

Here we see God sitting upon His throne. Suddenly as Daniel watches a brilliant, flaming figure steps before God. It is none other than Jesus—the great attorney of this heavenly court. "My little children, these things write I unto you, that ye sin not. And if any man sin, we have an advocate (an attorney) with the Father, Jesus Christ, the righteous." 1 John 2:1.

Here is Jesus, our lawyer, our interceder, accompanied by all the holy angels as witnesses gathered before God, the judge. Then, the Judgment began and the books were opened. What books are opened? "The books were opened: and another book was opened, which is the book of life: and the dead were judged out of those things which were written in the books, according to their works." Revelation 20:12.

Friend, we must be sure that our name is written in the book of life. Accept Jesus Christ NOW as your personal Saviour and your name will be written there.

Will all be saved whose names are once placed in the book? No, and that is what is so sad. "He that overcometh, the same shall be clothed in white raiment; and I will not blot out his name out of the book of life, but I will confess his name before my Father, and before his angels." Revelation 3:5.

Those who have once followed Jesus, but have wandered away and not returned, their names will be blotted out of the book when the judgment work is being done.

Secrets Revealed In Judgment

Everything will figure in the judgment. It gives us a little idea of how solemn that work is as we read, "But I say unto you, That every idle word that men shall speak, they shall give account thereof in the day of judgment." Matthew 12:36. The angels have a faithful record of every word and act.

These are solemn days in which we are living. And God is expecting more of His people than in any other time. The days of ignorace He winked at (Acts 17:30, 31), but He is asking His people now to repent, for He is lighting the earth with His special message of Present Truth.

In Ecclesiastes 12:13 and 14 we find, "Let us hear the conclusion of the whole matter: Fear God, and keep his commandments: for this is the whole duty of man. For God shall bring every work into judgment, with every secret thing, whether it be good, or whether it be evil." Sin may be concealed, denied, covered up from father, mother, wife, children, and associates; no one but the guilty actor may cherish the least suspicion of the wrong; but it is laid bare before the intelligences of heaven.

There are many people parading around in the cloak of religion and may be hiding from the world the things of the heart, but in the day of judgment, that ALL-SEEING EYE will detect every single thing—even the secret things.

Standard of the Judgment: God's Law

In the judgment you will have to face the Book. We will not be called on to live up to anything that is not written here, but we will face what IS written. Let us study the examination questions. We are plainly told what the questions will be. "For whosoever shall keep the whole law, and yet offend in one point, he is guilty of all. For he that said, Do not commit adultery, said also, Do not kill. Now if thou commit no adultery, yet if thou kill, thou art become a transgressor of the law. So speak ye, and so do, as they that shall be judged by the law of liberty." James 2:10-12. The law of God is the great standard of the judgment.

There are so many who think they will have a pull in that heavenly court. Many think they will explain it to God. "I know it says this or that," people tell me, "but I just can't do it. I'll explain it to God." O Friend, if there is to be any confessing made, it must be now! "If we confess our sins, he is faithful and just to forgive us our sins, and to cleanse us from all unrighteousness." 1 John 1:9.

Jesus has a wonderful way of dealing with sin. May God help us to get our hearts right with Him today and make an absolute surrender of everything within. When Jesus grips the springs of your heart, the life will be different.

Destiny of Every Soul Decided

This moment is big with destiny for every soul. Instead of the judgment being away in the future, that high tribunal is even now handing down its decisions of life and death. Shall we witness what happened as the investigative judgment began? God the Father is seated upon His glorious throne. Righteousness, truth, and justice center in Him. But unutterable love and mercy mingle with that justice. The angels stand in beautiful array on every side and Jesus Christ in all His beauty stands to plead for the race He died to redeem.

The record book is open and the lives of all come in review. Beginning with the first, our Advocate presents the cases of each successive generation, closing with the living. Names are accepted and retained in the Book of Life. Names are rejected. When there are sins remaining, unrepented of and unforgiven, their names will be blotted out of the Book of Life. Exodus 32:33.

There is Adam's name. There is the record that he disobeyed God. But there is also the record of forgiveness and pardon. Jesus immediately steps in between the record book and God the Father. He holds out His hands and says, "My blood, Father, My blood. Adam accepted Me, and My sacrifice pays his sin-debt." And all heaven rings out, "Keep his name on," and his name is kept on the record.

Down through the years, generation after generation, name after name is brought before the judgment. Then Saul's name is read. He started out to be a good king but soon pride filled his heart. Coveting, stealing, and lying followed, and there is no record of repentance or pardon. No doubt Jesus hung His head when all this came in review. He could not say, "My blood, My blood." The name is blotted out of the book.

We come to the perfect page. Not a sin recorded. And every individual can have his name transcribed on that page if he will. Jesus lived the life and shed His blood that we might be saved. All we need to do is to yield our all to Him and His perfection will stand in the place of our failures.

And down through the years the work progresses

until finally the judgment turns to care for the living. No one knows just when that will take place. But one of these days MY NAME will come up. I know pretty well just how the record stands. Yes, there is sin listed, for "all have sinned and come short of the glory of God." But, thank God, there is pardon registered. I have made certain of that. Just a few moments ago I claimed the promise of 1 John 1:9. My friend, how about you? Yes, you have sinned. Have you confessed that sin? Have you repented of your sins and asked Jesus to forgive?

Someday soon the last page of record will be opened. Someone's name is inscribed there. Whose it is, I do not know. For more than 100 years that work has been going on. How long it will continue I do not know. Christ could not have come before 1844, but now He can come anytime. When the last soul is sealed for eternity, Jesus will stand up in the courts of heaven and hold out His blood stained arms that have been reaching out for sinners all these years and He will announce, "IT IS DONE." "He that is unjust, let him be unjust still . . . he that is righteous, let him be righteous still."

My friend, the way is open today to place your case in Jesus' hands. God says, "Now is the accepted time . . . now is the day of salvation." 2 Corinthians 6:2.

Friend, this shows very clearly that there will come a time when it will be too late to be accepted. There will come a time when salvation will no longer be offered. The last appeal will have been made; the last sermon will have been preached; the last soul saved. If I know your heart, my friend, I believe you desire above everything else to put your life in Jesus' hands fully NOW before probation closes. This moment can be your moment of decision. And may God bless you.

AVAILABLE BOOKS

Listed below are the books written by *The Quiet Hour* speakers that are still in print. Suggested donation price is shown.

Written by J. L. Tucker

B-011 A Man Called Benaiah / 45c
B-111 And God Spared Not . . . / 45c
B-004 Angels and Their Ministry / 45c
B-022 Another Look at the Christian Sabbath / $1.50
B-016 Bones in the Church / 50c
B-015 Building a Happy Home / 45c
B-028 Devotional Guide / 50c
B-147 Devotional Guide, Vol. 44 / 50c
B-031 Elijah—The Man for This Crisis Hour / 45c
B-077 Give Me a Mountain / 50c
B-041 God in the Shadows / 45c
B-043 God's Great Questions to Man / 50c
B-093 God's Precious Promises / 45c
B-146 Heart Religion / 45c
B-076 How Are the Mighty Fallen! / 45c
B-121 I Climbed Mt. Sinai—God's Ten Rules for Peace of Mind / $1.00
B-137 I Walked Where Jesus Walked / 50c
B-010 In the Beginning God / 50c
B-055; -056; -057; -058; -059; -060 Inspirational Poems,
    Vols. 2-6, 8 / 50c each
B-136 Into All the World / 45c
B-050 It Happened at Night / 45c
B-028 Jehovah's Witnesses / 10c (Tract)
B—061 Jesus / 45c
B-062 John—A Man Sent From God / 45c
B-154 Lesson From the Life and Teachings of Apostle Paul / 50c
B-069 Looking Unto Jesus / 45c
B-034 Maintaining a Christian Experience / 45c
B-081 Opening of the Heart to God / 50c (Mrs. J. L.)
B-082 Our Lord's Return / 45c
B-083 Our Wonderful Bible / 75c
B-084 Our Wonderful Jesus / 75c
B-134 Other Women to be Remembered / 50c
B-086; -087; -088; -089; -090; -091; Poems We Love,
    Vols., 4-8, & 10 / 50c each
B-100 Quiet Hour Sermons / 45c
B-101 Quiet Hour Sermons, Vol. 3 / 45c
B-102 Quiet Hour Talks / 45c
B-009 Revelation Beatitudes of Jesus / 45c
B-032 Some Absolute Essentials / 45c
B-024 Study Notes on the Book of Daniel / $1.50
B-108 Study Notes on the Book of Revelation / $2.00
B-008 The Beast and His Mark / 50c
B-027 The Devil and His Devices / 45c
B-046 The Gospel and What It Saves Us From / 50c
B-054 The Great I Am / 55c
B-066 The King Is Coming / 45c
B-094 The Lord Is My Shepherd / 50c

B-038 The Man Who Played the Fool / 45c
B-063 The Man Who Tried to Run From God / 45c
B-073 The Master and His Friends / 45c
B-123; -124; -129 Treasured Gleanings, Vols. 2-4 / 50c each
B-126 Triumphant Living / 45c
B-001 What a Man! (Abraham) / 45c
B-030 When a Man Dies, What Then? / 75c
B-133 Women To Be Remembered / 45c
B-099 Your Questions Answered From the Bible / 45c

Written by L. E. Tucker

B-039 A Day of Freedom / 50c
B-002 African Safari / 75c
B-145 Are Love and Sex Enough / 75c
B-109 Are You Saved? / 45c
B-007 Baptized With the Holy Spirit / 50c
B-033 Coming World Events / 50c
B-028 Devotional Guide, Vol. 43 / 50c
B-006 End of the World Final Events / $1.50
B-157 Finding God Through the Sanctuary / $2.00
B-049 From Dust to Glory / $5.00
B-136 Into All the World / 45c
B-068 Is There Life After Life? / 45c
B-141 Living Temples / $1.00
B-003 Man: By Evolution or By Special Creation? / 45c
B-080 Nutrition and Health / $1.00
B-150 Nutrition and Health, Volume 2 / $1.00
B-097 Prophecy and the Cross / 50c
B-095 Psychics and Prophets / 50c
B-115; -116 Satanic Spectacular, Vols. 1 & 2 / 45c each
B-125 Speaking in Tongues / 45c
B-078 The Last Night on Earth / 45c
B-020 Visit to the Cannibals & Other Stories / 45c
B-025 Who Shall Decide? / 45c
B-118 Why Suffering? / 45c
B-051 Would You Like to Be Healed? / 50c

A 30% discount is suggested on any order of 25 or more books of one title in this section to one address in the USA.

Tiny Giant Series—40 Missionary Boooklets / 15 cents each; entire series of 40 different titles, $5.00.

Search Series—Pastor LaVerne E. Tucker's evangelistic messages in booklet form; 40 different topics, 40 booklets at 15 cents each; the entire series, $5.00.

A 50% discount is suggested on any order of one box (approximately 500 booklets) of one title of the Tiny Giant or Search series of booklets to one address in the USA.

A 40% discount is suggested on any order of 25 or more booklets of one title of the Tiny Giant or Search series to one address in the USA; a 20% discount for Canadian orders.

The Quiet Hour, Redlands, California 92373 USA

The Quiet Hour Cassettes

(Please order by number)

by LaVERNE TUCKER

CS-1 The World's Greatest Love Story / Time's Last Minute
CS-2 Love, Sex, and Marriage / How Jesus Can Be More Real
CS-3 Sudden Invasion From Outer Space / Heaven is for Real
CS-4 How You Can be Sure You Are Ready for Heaven /
     The True Lord's Day — Saturday or Sunday?
CS-5 Why Christians Keep Sunday /
     BLOOD AND SNOW on the Streets of Your Town
CS-6 Our Beloved Dead / The Truth About HELL FIRE
CS-7 The Bible's Greatest Time Prophecy /
     The Great Judgment Day
CS-8 How to Find God's True Church Today /
     How to Postpone Your Own Funeral
CS-9 Power for Living the Victorious Life /
     The Mark of the Beast
CS-10 What is the Unpardonable Sin? /
     DISCOVERED: A Peculiar People
CS-11 The Coming Battle of Armageddon /
     How to Build a Daring Faith
CS-12 Why God Allows Suffering and Trials /
     Appointment in Heaven
CS-13 The Finished Task / Scars vs Eternal Pleasures
CS-14 Modern Prophets—Are They of God? (J. Smith,
     Jeane Dixon, Ellen White)
CS-15 Speaking in Tongues /
     Baptized With the Holy Spirit
CS-16 The Last Night on Earth /
     When Will the Last Night Be?
CS-17 The Truth About Exorcism /
     Can the Dead Communicate with the Living?
CS-18 Satanic Spectacular: Why Seek the Spectacular? /
     What Spiritism Teaches
CS-19 The Faith That Heals /
     CHRIST—The Mediator in All Ages
CS-20 Strategy for Stress Control /
     Why Be a Vegetarian?
CS-21 Who Are the 144,000? / Partnership With God
CS-22 Does the Bible Teach a Pre-Tribulation Rapture? /
     The Rich Man and Lazarus

by J. L. TUCKER

CT-1 When Days Are Dark / Be Not Afraid
CT-2 The Haunted Heart / Salvation—Free to All
CT-3 Give God a Chance / Just Being Happy
CT-4 What Jesus is to Me / Time Is Running Out
CT-5 Wonders of Bible Prophecy /
     Seven Women After One Man
CT-6 Pastor J. L. Tucker's Favorite Chapters of the Bible
CT-7 Favorite Chapters, No. 2

CT-8   Poems We Love, No. 1
CT-9   Poems We Love, No. 2
CT-10 Bones in the Church, No. 1
CT-11 Bones in the Church, No. 2
CT-12 The Lord is My Shepherd, No. 1
CT-13 The Lord is My Shepherd, No. 2

The Quiet Hour Radiobroadcast

A cassette of ANY Quiet Hour radiobroadcast is available. BE SURE to give both date of program heard and title of sermon presented.

Suggested donation for each cassette: $2.50
PLEASE ALLOW 4-8 weeks for delivery!

CASSETTE ALBUMS

Pastor J. L. Tucker and Pastor LaVerne E. Tucker have prepared the following cassette albums that will be a blessing and an encouragement.

CA-1 I Climbed Mt. Sinai, by J. L. Tucker, has now been narrated on 8 cassettes. Included in the handsomely bound vinyl case with the cassettes is the book by the same title. You will thrill with Pastor Tucker's climb of Mt. Sinai, the studies of law and grace, and the discussion of each of the Ten Commandments. Studies on What was nailed to the cross? and The New Commandment complete the series. Price $20.

CA-2 That Book in the Attic. Narrated by J. L. Tucker, included in the beautiful vinyl case are four cassettes and *that* book which was found in the attic—an attractive paperback edition of *Daniel and Revelation,* by Uriah Smith. This thrilling story by Helen Oswald will prove to be a rich blessing. Price $15.

CA-3 Another Look at the Christian Sabbath is narrated by J. L. Tucker. Included in the vinyl case with the 4 cassettes is the 100-page book by the same title, written by Pastor Tucker. Price $15.

CA-4 Finding God Through the Sanctuary, by Morris D. Lewis and LaVerne E. Tucker, is narrated by Pastor LaVerne E. Tucker. Here is a compilation of the 13 Search television programs with Pastor Lewis and the Tuckers on the subject of the sanctuary, plus a prophecy study by Pastor Tucker on "The Cleansing of the Sanctuary." This cassette series is far more complete than the radiobroadcast version and includes the songs used on the telecast. Included in the vinyl case with the 4 cassettes (C-90s) is the 130-page book by the same title. Price $15, postage paid.

THE QUIET HOUR • Redlands, California 92373

MUSIC ALBUMS
CASSETTES, RECORDS, and 8-TRACKS

QH-1001 God Loves You and other favorites by the Tucker Family Singers—Pastor Bill Tucker and Pastor and Mrs. LaVerne Tucker.

Song titles: God Loves You; Fill My Cup, Lord; The Wonder of It All; If Christ Should Come Tonight; Redemption Draweth Nigh; Reach Out to Jesus; Oh, It Is Wonderful; Search; Jesus Is Coming Again; I Am Looking Today for Him; Ever Gentle, Ever Sweet; This Love Is Mine; Resting in His Love; Who Killed Jesus?

Price: $7 for stereo cassettes and stereo records; $8 for 8-track stereos; (Canada and foreign, add $1).

QH-1002 Tucker Family Favorites adds three additional singers—Pastor John Tucker, and Chad and Amy, children of Bill and Jackie Tucker. Organist and pianist is Jackie Hiser Tucker; orchestra arranged and conducted by Wayne Hooper.

Titles: In the Garden; Those Nails Were Mine; The Carpenter; Oh, Friend Do You Love Jesus; For Those Tears I Died; The Longer I Serve Him; Thank You Jesus; I'll Tell the World; Peace That My Saviour Has Given; Never Give Up; Day by Day; Like Jesus.

Price: $7 for stereo records and stereo cassettes; $8 for 8-track stereo; (Canada and foreign, add $1).

QH-1003 OLD TIME FAVORITES with the Tuckers features Dona Klein at the console of the new Rogers organ at The Quiet Hour studios, the lovely baritone solos by Bill Tucker, duets by Bill and Alma Tucker, and trios by Bill, Alma and LaVerne Tucker.

Titles are: Marching to Zion; Only Trust Him; Wonderful Peace/Peace Like a River; My Jesus, I Love Thee/I Love Thee; The Old Rugged Cross; Love Lifted Me; Sunshine in the Soul/Heavenly Sunshine; Anywhere With Jesus; Near the Cross/At the Cross; Count Your Blessings; and Pass Me Not.

Price: $7 for stereo records and cassettes; $8 for 8-track stereo; (Canada and foreign, add $1).

QH-1004 JESUS and Other Songs by the TUCKER FAMILY SINGERS with orchestration by Calvin Taylor,and features the rich baritone voice of Bill Tucker as soloist. Amy and Chad join with their daddy, Bill Tucker, in one song; Alma and LaVerne join with Bill in two songs; and Alma and Bill do one duet.

Titles are: Jesus; He Touched Me; I Found the Answer; I'll Be a Friend of His; More of You; You're Something Special; Jesus Is All the World to Me; Only Jesus Can Satisfy Your Soul; I'd Rather Have Jesus; A Man Named Jesus.

Price: $7 for stereo record and cassettes; $8 for 8-track stereos (Canada and foreign, add $1).

THE QUIET HOUR, Redlands, California 92373

HOME BIBLE STUDIES
On Videocassettes

The Search telecast videocassettes are proving to be an excellent aid to Home Bible Studies. All you need is your own TV, a videocassette player, and our Search telecast videocassettes.

Any combination of videocassettes may be purchased to suit the needs of your home or Bible study group. The Search telecast format is conducted in the home of Pastor and Mrs. LaVerne Tucker, with their friends. And your Bible study group will have a seat with them at each meeting. Best of all, you can stop at anytime and review a point until it is clearly understood.

Viewing a 30-minute Search for Truth program in color on a vital Bible subject will add a new dimension to your own spiritual growth and that of your family and friends. It is proving to be just the needed stimulus for a continuing search for truth. Here is your golden opportunity.

To make sure that you get the most for your small investment, we have packaged four half-hour Bible studies on a two-hour videocassette. Listed below are just a few of the 110 topics available. Write for our latest Cassette Catalog. Choose the videocassette package(s) you desire, state either Beta or VHS type desired, list the videocassette numbers (such as, VC-24 through VC-27), and send your personal check or money order to:

THE QUIET HOUR
Personal Video Ministries
Redlands, CA 92373

VIDEOCASSETTE TITLES

_____VC-12 The Last Night on Earth
When Will Be the Last Night on Earth?
Facing the Future Without Fear
The World's Greatest Love Story
_____VC-13 Practicing the Presence of Jesus
The Challenge of the Hour
Do You Have Eternal Life?
Transformed Living Temples—Part 1
_____VC-14 Food and Emotional Health
Right Food for 21st Century Living
What's Wrong With Refined Foods
Prevention of Heart Disease
_____VC-15 Weight Control
Prevention of Hypoglycemia and Diabetes
Prevention of Cancer
Would You Like to Be Healed?

Dr. Graham Maxwell Series:

_____VC-17 All God Asks of Us Is Trust
The Meaning of Faith
You Can Trust the Bible
You Can Trust the Translations
_____VC-18 You Can Trust the Versions
You Can Understand the Meaning
God's Respect for Us Sinners
Worshipping God Without Fear
_____VC-19 (More of Dr. Maxwell Series
Available July 1982)

The Compleat Marriage Series with Nancy and Harry Van Pelt:

_____VC-20 The State of Marriage Today
Meeting Your Mate's Needs
Accepting Your Mate
Communicating with Your Mate
_____VC-21 Understanding Your Mate
The Roles in Marriage
Sexually Fulfilling Your Mate
Having Fun With Your Mate

Nutrition and Health Series #2 with Dr. and Mrs. U. D. Register:

_____VC-22 How to Prevent Heart Disease
Pregnancy and Nutriton by Pat Johnson
How to Help Prevent Cancer
People of China and Nutrition
_____VC-23 Diet and Nutrition for the Golden Years
Fiber in the Diet
(TWO MORE TOPICS TO COME)

Sanctuary Series with M. D. Lewis:

_____VC-24 Christ's Relation to the Sanctuary
Christ the Door
Behold the Lamb
Christ in the Court
_____VC-25 Entering the Holy Place
Furniture in the Holy Place
The Walls of Salvation
Into the Holiest Place
_____VC-26 Blood on the Altars
Pattern of the Heavenly Sanctuary
The Priest Taken from Among Men
Breastplate and Precious Stones
_____VC-27 The Sanctuary Summarized

_____VC-28 Can the Dead Communicate with the Living?

**PRICES: ½ inch BETA-2 hours (4 programs), $40
½ inch VHS-2 hours (4 programs), $40**
PLEASE ALLOW 4-6 WEEKS FOR DELIVERY

SEARCH • Redlands, California 92373